INVENTORS WHO CHANGED THE WORLD

THOMAS EDISON
WIZARD OF LIGHT AND SOUND

AMY GRAHAM

MyReportLinks.com Books
an imprint of

 Enslow Publishers, Inc. **E**
Box 398, 40 Industrial Road
Berkeley Heights, NJ 07922
USA

MyReportLinks.com Books, an imprint of Enslow Publishers, Inc. MyReportLinks®
is a registered trademark of Enslow Publishers, Inc.

Library of Congress Cataloging-in-Publication Data

Graham, Amy.
  Thomas Edison : wizard of light and sound / Amy Graham.
     p. cm. — (Inventors who changed the world)
  Includes bibliographical references and index.
  ISBN-13: 978-1-59845-052-1
  ISBN-10: 1-59845-052-2
  1. Edison, Thomas A. (Thomas Alva), 1847–1931—Juvenile literature. 2. Inventors—United States—
Biography—Juvenile literature. 3. Scientists—United States—Biography—Juvenile literature. 4.
Sound—Recording and reproducing—Juvenile literature. I. Title.
TK140.E3G72 2006
621.3092—dc22
[B]
                              2006022284

Printed in the United States of America

10 9 8 7 6 5 4 3 2 1

To Our Readers:
Through the purchase of this book, you and your library gain access to the Report Links that specifically
back up this book.
The Publisher will provide access to the Report Links that back up this book and will keep these Report
Links up to date on **www.myreportlinks**.com for five years from the book's first publication date.
We have done our best to make sure all Internet addresses in this book were active and appropriate when
we went to press. However, the author and the Publisher have no control over, and assume no liability
for, the material available on those Internet sites or on other Web sites they may link to.
The usage of the MyReportLinks.com Books Web site is subject to the terms and conditions stated on the
Usage Policy Statement on **www.myreportlinks.com.**
A password may be required to access the Report Links that back up this book. The password is found
on the bottom of page 4 of this book.
Any comments or suggestions can be sent by e-mail to comments@myreportlinks.com or to the address
on the back cover.

Photo Credits: Alexander Graham Bell National Historic Site, p. 60; American Heritage Inc., p. 90;
Chautauqua Institution, p. 71; Charles Edison Fund, p. 74; Earlycinema.com, p. 113; Edison Electric
Institute, p. 64; Federal Communications Commission, p. 32; GNU Free Documentation License, pp. 3,
8–9, 22–23, 37, 56–57, 75, 89; John Casale, p. 44; Library of Congress, pp. 1, 5, 10–11, 24, 31, 38–39,
48–49, 52–53, 58–59, 68, 70, 72, 79, 82–83, 84, 94–95, 103, 108, 112; Mississippi State University
Department of Electrical and Computer Engineering, p. 88; MyReportLinks.com Books, p. 4; National
Academy of Engineering, p. 67; National Archives, p. 77; National Park Service, pp. 14, 76, 86, 91;
PBS/WGBH, p. 12; Photos.com, pp. 1, 35; ShutterStock, pp. 62–63, 98–99; Smithsonian Institution,
p. 46; Smithsonian National Museum of American History, pp. 20, 106; Stock Ticker Company, p. 42; The
Edison Birthplace Museum, p. 25; The Henry Ford, pp. 47, 104; The Institution of Engineering and
Technology, p. 16; The Royal Institution of Great Britain, p. 41; Thomas A. Edison Papers—Rutgers
University, p. 93; Thomas Edison & Henry Ford Winter Estates, Inc., p. 97; University of Michigan Digital
Library Text Collections, p. 29; USPTO, p. 19; World Wide School, p. 26.

Cover Photo: Library of Congress; Photos.com

CONTENTS

MyReportLinks.com Books
Great Books, Great Links, Great for Research!

The Internet sites featured in this book can save you hours of research time. These Internet sites—we call them **"Report Links"**—are constantly changing, but we keep them up to date on our Web site.

When you see this "Approved Web Site" logo, you will know that we are directing you to a great Internet site that will help you with your research.

Give it a try! Type **http://www.myreportlinks.com** into your browser, click on the series title and enter the password, then click on the book title, and scroll down to the Report Links listed for this book.

The Report Links will bring you to great source documents, photographs, and illustrations. MyReportLinks.com Books save you time, feature Report Links that are kept up to date, and make report writing easier than ever! A complete listing of the Report Links can be found on pages 116–117 at the back of the book.

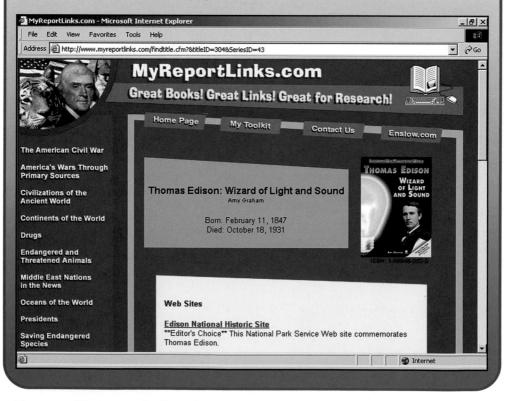

Please see "To Our Readers" on the copyright page for important information about this book, the MyReportLinks.com Web site, and the Report Links that back up this book.

Please enter **TEL1787** if asked for a password.

I have far more respect for the person with a single idea who gets there than for the person with a thousand ideas who does nothing.

—Thomas Edison

IMPORTANT DATES

1847—*February 11:* Born in Milan, Ohio.

1854—Moves with his family to Port Huron, Michigan.

1859—Takes a job as a newsboy on a train at age twelve.

1863 –1868—Works as a telegrapher around the United States and Canada.

1868—Applies for his first patent for a vote recorder in Boston.

1869—Moves to New York and invents improved stock ticker.

1871—Marries Mary Stilwell.

1876—Builds a laboratory in Menlo Park, New Jersey.

1877—Discovers a way to record and replay sound; invents the phonograph.

1879—Invents the incandescent light bulb.

1882—Opens the world's first central power station in New York City .

1884—Wife Mary dies; Edison left a widower with three young children.

1886—Marries second wife Mina Miller; moves to West Orange, New Jersey.

1888—Applies for a patent for the kinetoscope.

1889—Opens unsuccessful low-grade iron ore mine in Ogden, New Jersey.

1891—Displays first motion pictures on the peep-hole kinetoscope.

1893—Constructs world's first motion picture studio.

1895
–1896 —Experiments with X-rays until exposed workers fall sick.

1900
–1910 —Works on an improved battery for electric cars.

1914—Edison's West Orange Phonograph Works burns in a fire.

1915—Agrees to head the U.S. Naval Consulting Board.

1916—Takes first of several camping trips with Henry Ford and others.

1923—Searches for a source of natural rubber.

1929—Attends a celebration of the fiftieth anniversary of the lightbulb.

1931—*October 18:* Edison dies.

THE WIZARD OF MENLO PARK

CHAPTER 1

Everyone wanted to be first to board the train. It was New Year's Eve, 1879. The passengers were going to a New Year's Eve party unlike any other. As the packed train left the station, it let out a shrill whistle blast. The train puffed along, gaining speed as it went. It was bound for the New Jersey countryside. Tonight there was a grand occasion in the sleepy village of Menlo Park, the home of young inventor Thomas Edison. Just a year ago, he had awed people with his phonograph, an amazing machine that could record the human voice. Then it could play the voice back. It was the first time in the history of the world that sound had been recorded. Tonight he would display his latest invention: the lightbulb. The public was welcome. The excited crowds wanted to see for themselves the great miracle of electric light. It would change the world.

⊝ AN EVENING TO REMEMBER

The train pulled into the Menlo Park station. Steam hissed as it ground to a halt. The doors opened and passengers disembarked. The crowd gasped at the marvelous sight. Lights lined the street. Electric lamps hung from trees and poles. The lamps had wires that led to a generator that supplied the power. This was very different from the streetlights of the day. Gas lights lit the city streets of America. These electric lanterns were different. They gave off a pleasant light and did not flicker or grow dim. Gas lamps could grow dangerously hot, but Edison's lamps did not. His lamps did not release smelly, poisonous gases. Edison's laboratory was radiantly lit with twenty-five electric lamps. Other electric lights lit up Edison's office and nearby houses.

Three thousand people joined the throng that evening. They filled the streets of the small town. The mob crowded into the workshop where Edison told them about his new lightbulb. They watched in awe. Which was more exciting: a view of the new electric light, or a glimpse of the inventor? Which person was Edison? Such a genius would be easy to spot. He would be a dignified man wearing fine clothes and acting like a gentleman.[1] Edison did not fit the bill. Ladies and gentleman strolled about the laboratory dressed up. Edison did not. He wore simple clothes that were stained with chemicals. Edison talked plainly and was easy to understand. Then there was the matter of his age. His workers

Groundbreaking inventor Thomas Edison at his lab in West Orange, New Jersey.

The American Experience | Edison's Miracle of LIght - Microsoft Internet Explorer

File   Edit   View   Favorites   Tools   Help

Address http://www.pbs.org/wgbh/amex/edison/index.html

PBS HOME   PROGRAMS A-Z   TV SCHEDULES   SUPPORT PBS   SHOP PBS   SEARCH PBS

AMERICAN EXPERIENCE   KIDS | HOME

THE FILM & MORE
SPECIAL FEATURES
TIMELINE
GALLERY
TEACHER'S GUIDE

Edison's
Miracle
of Light

He harnessed electricity and revolutionized the world

Edison's Miracle of Light Web site allows access to early Edison sound recordings, such as "Mary Had a Little Lamb," performed by the inventor himself. An article on the difference between AC/DC currents is available, as is a time line of Edison's life, with photographs.

EDITOR'S CHOICE

called him "the Old Man" but Edison was just thirty-two.

When people think of Edison, they think of the lightbulb. Did you know that Edison was not the first person to make a lightbulb? Humans had tried to make an electric light for years. Some had even made lightbulbs, but they did not work very well. Edison figured it out. With this accomplishment, he secured his fame as the greatest American inventor. He did not stop there. Edison kept inventing throughout his long life. His inventions made him a wealthy man. He was not inventing for money. He always put his money toward new inventions.

➔ LIFE BEFORE THE AGE OF ELECTRICITY

Edison's inventions changed life in many ways. Some say he invented the future. Let us imagine what life was like in the mid-1800s, before Edison changed the world with his ideas. Picture a dark winter's night. You sit at your table and read by the dim glow of candlelight. The night's darkness fills the corners of the room. A kerosene lamp chases away the shadows near your father's chair. After a hard day's work, he reads the newspaper to learn about world events. A fire roars in the wood-stove. Your grandmother moves her rocking chair closer to the stove to warm herself while she knits. The room is quiet. The only sound is the swoosh of the broom as your mother sweeps the crumbs from the floorboards. If you want to hear music, you will have to get out your fiddle and play it yourself. There are no tape cassettes, CDs, computers, or iPods. Edison has not yet invented a way to record sounds and music. There is no recording industry.

Let us say you wanted to hear a human voice. You would have to talk to someone there in the room. There is no such thing as a radio. Edison did not invent the radio, though he lived to hear one. The chairs in the parlor do not face a television.

T. A. EDISON.
Electric-Lamp.

No. 223,898. Patented Jan. 27, 1880.

This is the original diagram that Thomas Edison submitted to the USPTO to obtain a patent for his electric-lamp. The electric-lamp came to be known as the lightbulb.

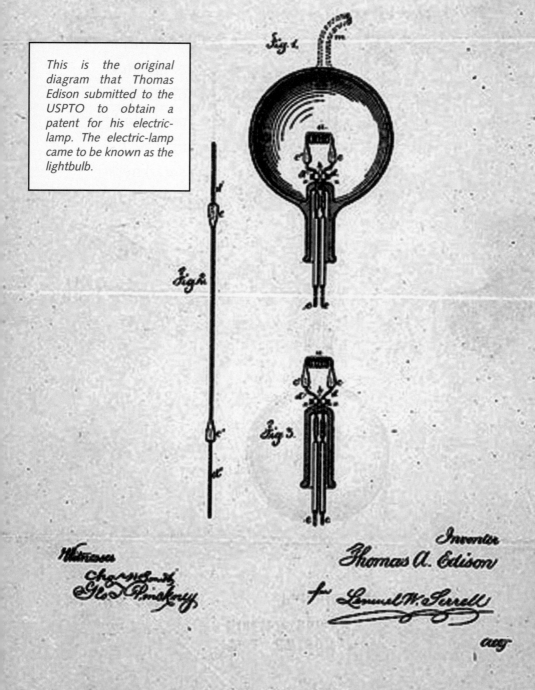

Witnesses

Chas H Smith
Geo T Pinckney

Inventor
Thomas A. Edison

for Lemuel W. Serrell

atty

There is no such thing. There are no movies to watch. Edison will make the first motion pictures in the 1890s. If you told someone back then that pictures would one day move and tell entertaining stories, they probably would not believe you.

Now imagine yourself walking away from the glow of the candlelight. Walk over to the window and lift back the curtain. You will see a cold sky full of bright stars. The dirt road outside is dark and silent at this time of night. During the day the road is busy. Horses trot along, kicking up dust, pulling carriages and wagons. There are no cars. When cars are invented, people call them "horseless carriages" at first. Edison will make an electric car. Turn and look out the window again. What is missing? No telephone poles line the dark street. That is right: Edison will even help to make the telephone. If this house is in town, there may be streetlights that are burning gas. The gas runs through pipes under the streets. The parlor may be lit with flickering gas lights. If the flame goes out accidentally, the poisonous gas fills the house. There is also the danger of an explosion. Luckily Edison's electric lightbulbs will put an end to these hazards.

Let us take a closer look around this house of the 1800s. Start in the kitchen. Grab your candle—it is dark in there. The room you see looks very different from your own kitchen. It is quiet, too. There is no electric hum. How do they keep

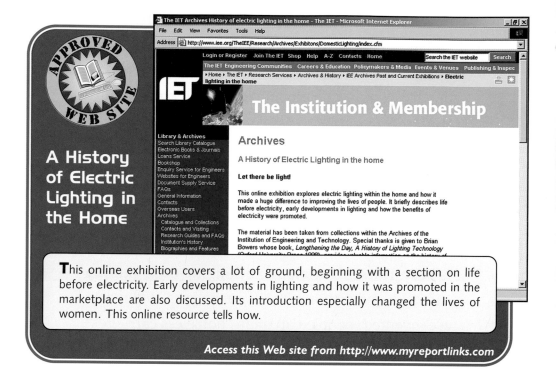

The IET Archives History of electric lighting in the home - The IET - Microsoft Internet Explorer

File   Edit   View   Favorites   Tools   Help

Address   http://www.iee.org/TheIEE/Research/Archives/Exhibitons/DomesticLighting/index.cfm

Login or Register   Join The IET Shop Help A-Z Contacts Home   Search the IET website   Search

The IET Engineering Communities   Careers & Education   Policymakers & Media   Events & Venues   Publishing & Inspec

▸ Home ▸ The IET ▸ Research Services ▸ Archives & History ▸ IEE Archives Past and Current Exhibitions ▸ Electric lighting in the home

IET

The Institution & Membership

Library & Archives
Search Library Catalogue
Electronic Books & Journals
Loans Service
Bookshop
Enquiry Service for Engineers
Websites for Engineers
Document Supply Service
FAQs
General Information
Contacts
Overseas Users
Archives
  Catalogue and Collections
  Contacts and Visiting
  Research Guides and FAQs
  Institution's History
  Biographies and Features

Archives

A History of Electric Lighting in the home

Let there be light!

This online exhibition explores electric lighting within the home and how it made a huge difference to improving the lives of people. It briefly describes life before electricity, early developments in lighting and how the benefits of electricity were promoted.

The material has been taken from collections within the Archives of the Institution of Engineering and Technology. Special thanks is given to Brian Bowers whose book, *Lengthening the Day, A History of Lighting Technology*

A History of Electric Lighting in the Home

This online exhibition covers a lot of ground, beginning with a section on life before electricity. Early developments in lighting and how it was promoted in the marketplace are also discussed. Its introduction especially changed the lives of women. This online resource tells how.

Access this Web site from http://www.myreportlinks.com

their food cold? They must do the dishes by hand. Where is the microwave? Wait—there are no appliances at all. This house has no wires. It has no outlets or switches. Edison has not yet found a way to deliver electricity to people's homes. The average person in the mid-1800s knew very little about electricity. An invisible source of energy that would one day power machines to lighten their chores at home? That would have sounded like the dreams of a madman.

⊜➔ A TIME OF GREAT CHANGE

When Edison was a boy, steam was king. Steam was a new source of energy. Trains ran on steam power. Their engines burned coal, and the coal fire made steam. Thanks to the new railroads, Americans settled the west. Trains carried supplies all across the country. Travel was faster than ever before. Then, in 1844, Samuel Morse invented the telegraph. Telegraph wires followed the train tracks. The telegraph was a new way to communicate. To send a message to a friend who lived far away, a person went to a telegraph office. There a person called a telegrapher took your message. He translated it into Morse code—a code made of short and long electrical impulses. The impulses traveled along a wire. Then a telegrapher at the receiving end would translate the code back into your message. A messenger would deliver the telegram to your friend's address. A telegraph was faster than sending a letter. America was on the brink of a great change. Science advanced quickly, thanks to Edison and others like him. Anything seemed possible.

⊜ INVENTING THE FUTURE

Boy, have times changed! What would your great-great-great grandparents think of life today? They would surely be amazed. The telegraph is no more. Now we use computers and cell phones to send messages in an instant. We owe thanks to Thomas Alva Edison who was born in 1847. As a boy, he watched the covered wagons on their way west. When he died in 1931, the world was a very different place. It was the age of electricity. Edison helped make that change. Edison did not go to the best schools. He hardly went to school at all. He did not attend college or even high school. By age twelve he had a full-time job. Yet, Edison did well in life. He became one of the most well-known and wealthiest people of his day. He made a career of inventing. Edison had patents for 1,093 inventions. This is more than any other person in American history.

Edison thought about things in a new way. Today we take his ideas for granted. It was not so during his lifetime. His ideas shocked people. There were rumors about him. Did he have magic powers? Maybe he was a wizard.[2] The phonograph, for example, absolutely amazed people. Edison was excited about the phonograph. He knew he had made history. He took it to New York City the day after he made it. He went to the offices of *Scientific American* and showed it off to the editor of the magazine. Soon throngs of people, wanting to hear the phonograph, crowded into the office. There were so many that the floor was in danger of collapsing.[3] A newspaper story dubbed Edison "the Wizard of Menlo Park." Soon everyone was talking about the Wizard. One April 1, there was a wild story in the newspapers. Edison had invented a new machine that would

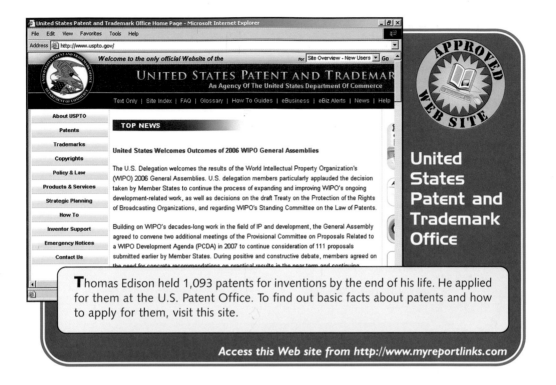

United States Patent and Trademark Office Home Page - Microsoft Internet Explorer

File Edit View Favorites Tools Help

Address http://www.uspto.gov/

Welcome to the only official Website of the

UNITED STATES PATENT AND TRADEMAR
An Agency Of The United States Department Of Commerce

Text Only | Site Index | FAQ | Glossary | How To Guides | eBusiness | eBiz Alerts | News | Help

About USPTO

Patents

Trademarks

Copyrights

Policy & Law

Products & Services

Strategic Planning

How To

Inventor Support

Emergency Notices

Contact Us

TOP NEWS

United States Welcomes Outcomes of 2006 WIPO General Assemblies

The U.S. Delegation welcomes the results of the World Intellectual Property Organization's (WIPO) 2006 General Assemblies. U.S. delegation members particularly applauded the decision taken by Member States to continue the process of expanding and improving WIPO's ongoing development-related work, as well as decisions on the draft Treaty on the Protection of the Rights of Broadcasting Organizations, and regarding WIPO's Standing Committee on the Law of Patents.

Building on WIPO's decades-long work in the field of IP and development, the General Assembly agreed to convene two additional meetings of the Provisional Committee on Proposals Related to a WIPO Development Agenda (PCDA) in 2007 to continue consideration of 111 proposals submitted earlier by Member States. During positive and constructive debate, members agreed on the need for concrete recommendations on practical results in the near term and continuing

United States Patent and Trademark Office

APPROVED WEB SITE

Thomas Edison held 1,093 patents for inventions by the end of his life. He applied for them at the U.S. Patent Office. To find out basic facts about patents and how to apply for them, visit this site.

Access this Web site from http://www.myreportlinks.com

end world hunger by feeding mankind. It was just a joke. April Fool's Day! People were fooled. It really did seem that Edison could do anything.

Then Edison made the lightbulb. People were sure he was a genius. His lamps glowed, but there was no flame. They ran on invisible energy. People compared Edison to Prometheus. The ancient Greeks told a story about Prometheus who stole fire from the gods. He gave the gift of fire to people. Edison was no magician. He was just a new kind of scientist ahead of his time. Before Edison, people studied science to understand the world around them. Edison was different—he was a

The Lemelson Center Presents... Edison Invents! – All about Thomas Edison and his inventions – Microsoft Internet Explorer

File   Edit   View   Favorites   Tools   Help

Address http://invention.smithsonian.org/centerpieces/edison/

The Lemelson Center Presents...

Edison Invents!

All about Thomas Edison and his inventions

Thomas Alva Edison changed our world! His genius gave us electric lights in our home and an entire system that produced and delivered electrical power. He was the first to record sound — and he also started the recording industry. Edison developed the first movie camera and produced the first movies. Learn more about this creative genius. You'll be "shocked" at what you discover!

Invention is 1% inspiration and 99% perspiration

Play Edison Invents!

The "Edison Invents" activity requires Flash. If you can see Edison's quotes, you have Flash. If you don't, download the free Flash plug-in.

Le___ __out Edison in these sections:

___ _ake a Light Bulb   Resources

___er for the Study of Invention and Innovation
___es © Smithsonian Institution ::: Privacy policy

Smithsonian

The Smithsonian presents **Edison Invents!,** about Thomas Edison and his inventions. Try the 'make a light bulb' experiment and play a matching activity game.

EDITOR'S CHOICE

practical scientist. He used science to solve problems. He invented products that helped people.

WHO CARES IF THEY LAUGH?

Edison did not care what people thought of him. He was happiest in the laboratory, where he could stay up half the night. He would catch a few hours of sleep on a workbench rather than return home. He was free to spit his tobacco juice on the floor. He did not have to shave or comb his hair. No one cared that his crumpled clothes were stained with chemicals. Edison loved to solve problems and was confident in his abilities. He was sure he could solve any problem with the right amount of hard work.

Edison was not afraid to take risks and try new things. He never let failure get him down. When Edison was an old man, he lost part of his laboratory. There was a fire during the night, and the flames quickly grew out of control. Luckily, no one was hurt. The buildings burned to the ground. Once the fire had died, Edison wandered through the rubble. He saw a photograph on the ground and reached down to rescue it. It was a picture of himself that had somehow escaped from the flames. "Never touched me!" he quipped.[4] Days later, he began to rebuild. He would make a better laboratory than ever before. Edison always looked at the bright side. His optimism helped him achieve great things.

"WHAT SEEMS IMPOSSIBLE TODAY MAY NOT BE TOMORROW"

E dison's boyhood is now a bit of a legend that has been told in countless books. There was even a movie about it produced in 1940. That is how entertaining it is. Edison was no different from most young boys. He liked to take things apart and see how they worked. He was full of energy and eager to take on challenges. He grew up to do amazing things. His story seems to say that anyone can succeed. One just has to try hard enough. Of course, not everyone is a genius like Edison.

Edison also knew how to tell a good story. In his old age, he wrote down his memories of his early years. His stories are often exciting and some are quite funny. One thing always comes through in his stories: Edison was a curious and hardworking boy.

CHAPTER

2

➜ FAMILY BACKGROUND

In 1730, a ship docked on the coast of New Jersey. It had sailed across the Atlantic from Holland. A little boy name John Edeson was on board. That little boy would become Thomas Edison's great grandfather. Edeson grew up in the American colonies and did

well for himself. He bought land and built a farm.
Other colonists were angry with England and
declared war on Great Britain. John Edeson did not
join the cause because he was happy with things as
they were. He had no complaint with the British.
The Americans won the war. Edeson found himself in a tough spot. He was accused of spying
for the British during the war. He sat in jail
for over a year before he was set free. He
was thankful to be alive and left
America to make a new home in
Canada. The British gave him 500
acres (202 hectares) on the island of
Nova Scotia.[1] The Edeson family
started with a clean slate. They even
changed the spelling of their name—
now they were the Edisons.

Thomas Edison's father left Canada
in a hurry in the dark of night. The army
was at his heels. Samuel Edison did not like
the British. He tried to overthrow the government. The uprising did not go well. Some of the
revolutionaries were put to death, but Sam
escaped. He fled on foot to America. He made his
way across the border into Michigan. For two
years he wandered and eventually found work in
the lumber trade. He bought a house in Milan,
Ohio, a booming merchant town. A canal ran

This image of Thomas Edison was taken when he was about thirty-three years old.

through the town that connected to the Huron River and then Lake Erie. The canal was a major trade route. Farmers brought their grain to Milan, and boats carried grain and lumber to the cities in the east. Sam Edison sent for his wife and family to join him.

⊛ A Star Is Born

Thomas Alva Edison was the baby of the family. His mother gave birth to him in Ohio on February 11, 1847. He was the seventh child of Sam and Nancy Elliott Edison. As a child everyone called

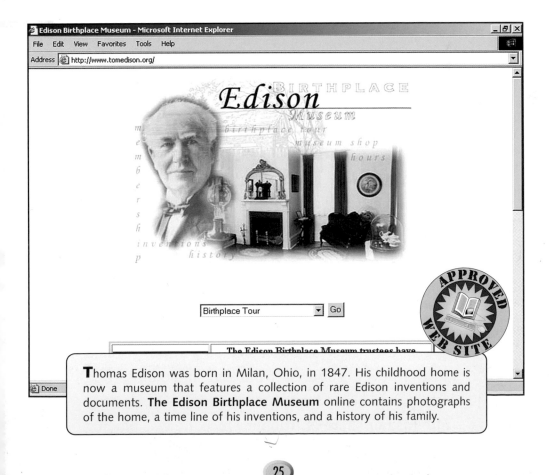

Thomas Edison was born in Milan, Ohio, in 1847. His childhood home is now a museum that features a collection of rare Edison inventions and documents. **The Edison Birthplace Museum** online contains photographs of the home, a time line of his inventions, and a history of his family.

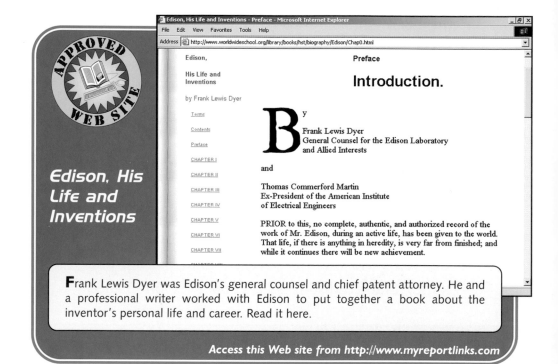

Edison, His Life and Inventions

Edison, His Life and Inventions - Preface - Microsoft Internet Explorer

File Edit View Favorites Tools Help

Address http://www.worldwideschool.org/library/books/hst/biography/Edison/Chap0.html

Edison,

His Life and
Inventions

by Frank Lewis Dyer

Terms

Contents

Preface

CHAPTER I

CHAPTER II

CHAPTER III

CHAPTER IV

CHAPTER V

CHAPTER VI

CHAPTER VII

Preface

Introduction.

By
Frank Lewis Dyer
General Counsel for the Edison Laboratory
and Allied Interests

and

Thomas Commerford Martin
Ex-President of the American Institute
of Electrical Engineers

PRIOR to this, no complete, authentic, and authorized record of the
work of Mr. Edison, during an active life, has been given to the world.
That life, if there is anything in heredity, is very far from finished; and
while it continues there will be new achievement.

Frank Lewis Dyer was Edison's general counsel and chief patent attorney. He and a professional writer worked with Edison to put together a book about the inventor's personal life and career. Read it here.

Access this Web site from http://www.myreportlinks.com

him "Alva." Sometimes they called him "Al" for short. Alva was raised much like an only child, for his siblings were much older than he was. Two of his brothers and one sister died before he was born. In the 1800s, it was a sad fact that families often lost children to disease. There have been great advances in medicine during the last century. Life today is much safer for American children. Sam and Nancy Edison must have been nervous about Alva. He was often sick as a child. He had scarlet fever, suffered from ear infections, and sometimes he had trouble breathing. He also got into his fair share of trouble. Once, he was playing on the rim of a grain elevator and fell in. Another time he had to be fished out of the canal.

→ MOVE TO MICHIGAN

The canal was the pride of the town of Milan. When the railroad company began to lay tracks in Ohio, the people of Milan rallied. They did not want the new railroad to go through their town. They thought the trains were noisy and dangerous. They did not want the railroad to compete with their canal. Due to their complaints, the railroad did not go through Milan. At first it seemed the townspeople had won the battle. In hindsight, it was a bad decision. While the canal lay covered in ice in the winter months, the trains chugged on. Soon most farmers and woodsmen shipped their products by train. The canal system fell into disrepair. Sam Edison was one of many people who decided to move away. He took his family to Port Huron, Michigan, when Alva was seven years old.

Sam Edison knew the town of Port Huron. He had passed through there when he first escaped to America. The town sits on the shore of Lake Huron. The St. Clair River enters the lake there, and it was a busy port town. The Edisons lived in a fine brick home near the edge of a military base. The family had been well-off back in Milan. Now they never had enough money. Sam Edison tried his hand at many different trades. He ran a grocery store, grew fruits and vegetables, worked in the lumber trade, and did carpentry. He was always looking for ways to make money. Beside their house he built a tall tower that came to be quite a tourist attraction. People called it the Lighthouse of Port Huron. Sam Edison charged a small fee to allow people to climb to the top to see the view. Young Alva watched his father try many different jobs. His father did not worry about money. He was always confident he could come up with the money they needed. Edison was the same when he grew up. He learned this from his father.[2]

⇒ AN ADDLED STUDENT

Alva's mother enrolled him in school when they reached Port Huron. Alva did not last long at the schoolhouse. Al frustrated his teacher. The boy was always daydreaming, and he doodled when he should have been listening. In those days, teachers lectured—students had to pay attention or else. One day Alva's teacher called him "addled." Al was hurt by the comment. His mother marched down to see the teacher and let her know that there was nothing wrong with her son. She removed Al from school and began to teach him herself. Nancy Edison had been a schoolteacher before she married. Edison was forever thankful to his mother. She taught him to love books and reading and she had great faith in him. Alva

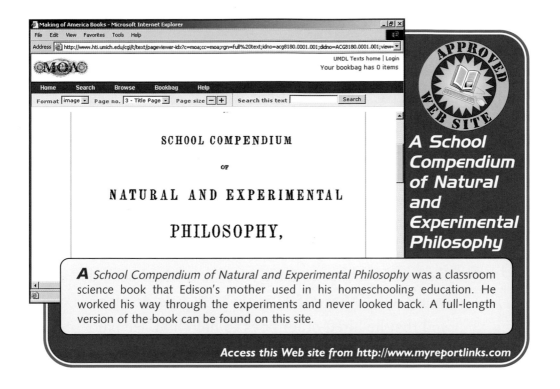

Making of America Books - Microsoft Internet Explorer

File   Edit   View   Favorites   Tools   Help

Address http://www.hti.umich.edu/cgi/t/text/pageviewer-idx?c=moa;cc=moa;rgn=full%20text;idno=acg8180.0001.001;didno=ACG8180.0001.001;view=

UMDL Texts home | Login
Your bookbag has 0 items

MOA

Home   Search   Browse   Bookbag   Help

Format [image] Page no. [3 - Title Page] Page size [-][+]   Search this text [   ] [Search]

SCHOOL COMPENDIUM

OF

NATURAL AND EXPERIMENTAL

PHILOSOPHY,

APPROVED WEB SITE

A School Compendium of Natural and Experimental Philosophy

A *School Compendium of Natural and Experimental Philosophy* was a classroom science book that Edison's mother used in his homeschooling education. He worked his way through the experiments and never looked back. A full-length version of the book can be found on this site.

Access this Web site from http://www.myreportlinks.com

always wanted to do his best. He liked to make his mother proud of him.[3] Nancy Edison bought her son a classroom science book called *A School Compendium of Natural and Experimental Philosophy* by Richard Green Parker. It would change the course of his life. Alva read the experiments and then tried to do them himself. He bought his own chemicals. He wrote "POISON" on the labels so that no one would disturb them.

GRAND TRUNK RAILROAD

At age twelve, Edison took his first job. The Grand Trunk Railroad now ran through Port Huron. Sam Edison got his son the job of candy butch. A candy butch walked the train aisles. He sold snacks, tobacco, and newspapers to the passengers. Al rode the train 60 miles (97 kilometers) south to Detroit each day. He started work at seven o'clock each morning and did not get home until after nine o'clock in the evening. Al kept busy during his six hour layovers in the city. He bought the evening newspapers and restocked his food supplies. He spent his free time reading at the Detroit Free Public library, which made his mother happy. She was reluctant to have Alva at work at such a young age.[4] After a few months Al was doing so well that he hired other boys to help him. He paid newsboys to sell papers on different trains. He paid other boys to run a newsstand and a farm stand selling fresh fruits and vegetables at the Port Huron train depot.

⊛ Newspaper Publisher

Al set up a laboratory on the train, and with his free time he did experiments. One day a chemical spilled and a fire broke out. The conductor was burned while putting out the flames. That was the end of the laboratory. Alva found something new to do. He started a newspaper that he printed himself on the train. The *Grand Trunk Herald* sold for three cents a copy. The paper lasted for about six months. It made a good profit, but setting the newsprint by hand was too slow and dull for Alva.

▲ Edison's first son, Thomas Edison, Jr., was born on January 10, 1876. When he got older his father asked him to change his last name because he had been selling the use of it to advertise quack medicines which embarrassed the family.

Around the age of twelve Alva's ears began to hurt and he could not hear very well. It got worse with time. Edison thought that a trainman had made him go deaf. The man grabbed hold of his ears to pull him aboard a moving train.[5] It is hard to know what really caused his hearing to go. The bad case of scarlet fever could have hurt his ears. Edison did not mind being hard of hearing. He always claimed that it led to his success as an inventor.[6] Noises did not distract him so he spent a lot of time with his own uninterrupted thoughts.

BATTLE OF SHILOH

The American Civil War broke out when Alva was fourteen years old. On April 6, 1862, Al arrived in

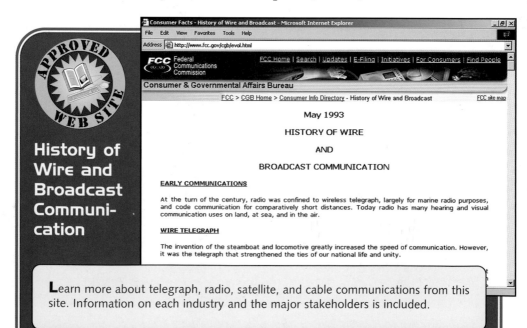

History of Wire and Broadcast Communication

Consumer Facts - History of Wire and Broadcast - Microsoft Internet Explorer

File   Edit   View   Favorites   Tools   Help

Address http://www.fcc.gov/cgb/evol.html

FCC Federal Communications Commission

FCC Home | Search | Updates | E-Filing | Initiatives | For Consumers | Find People

Consumer & Governmental Affairs Bureau

FCC > CGB Home > Consumer Info Directory - History of Wire and Broadcast   FCC site map

May 1993

HISTORY OF WIRE

AND

BROADCAST COMMUNICATION

EARLY COMMUNICATIONS

At the turn of the century, radio was confined to wireless telegraph, largely for marine radio purposes, and code communication for comparatively short distances. Today radio has many hearing and visual communication uses on land, at sea, and in the air.

WIRE TELEGRAPH

The invention of the steamboat and locomotive greatly increased the speed of communication. However, it was the telegraph that strengthened the ties of our national life and unity.

Learn more about telegraph, radio, satellite, and cable communications from this site. Information on each industry and the major stakeholders is included.

Access this Web site from http://www.myreportlinks.com

Detroit to pick up his newspapers. The headlines that day told of a huge battle. Thousands of soldiers lay dead and wounded. Al realized that many people on the train would want to read about the Battle of Shiloh. He only had enough money to buy his usual one hundred newspapers. He somehow talked the *Detroit Free Press* office into giving him one thousand papers on credit. When he returned to the train station, he spoke to the Detroit telegraph operator. He wired news of the battle up the line. At every stop on the ride home, people swarmed around him. They had heard the news and wanted to buy a paper. As his papers dwindled, Al raised the price. He made a small fortune that day. The experience gave him a new appreciation for the telegraph.[7]

➲ SENDING INFORMATION ELECTRONICALLY

Like many boys of the day, Al was fascinated with the telegraph. He memorized the dots and dashes of Morse code. He spent time at the railroad telegraph offices. He watched the telegraphers at work. One day, Al saved a three-year-old boy who had wandered on to the train tracks. The boy's father was grateful. As a reward, he offered to teach Al how to operate the telegraph. Al quickly agreed. Back at home, he strung up a telegraph wire to a friend's house. He taught his friend telegraphy as well. They communicated back and forth.

Alva practiced telegraphy eighteen hours a day and soon had it mastered.

Alva Edison took his first job as a telegrapher in 1863. He worked for Western Union. Their office was in downtown Port Huron. It was really just a corner of the jewelry store. He now pre-ferred people to call him by his true first name. Thomas Edison spent all day at the office. He stayed there at night, too. When the line was quiet, Edison was free to tinker. One day an exper-iment got out of hand. There was a loud bang. As loud bangs were bad for business, his boss asked him to find a new job.

⊜ ALWAYS TINKERING

For the next five years, Edison tramped around the United States and Canada. He found work as a telegrapher. All the while he worked to improve his skills. He wanted to be fast because fast teleg-raphers got the best jobs. Edison rigged up a machine to help him learn. The machine recorded incoming code. Then he could play the code back at a slower speed. Edison learned to write very small so he could write faster. Before long he was a top-rate telegrapher. To entertain himself, Edison played with the batteries, wires, and other equipment he found around the office. He also liked to play practical jokes. Once he glued down the transmitting keys. The next operator on duty

▲ *This is an image of an old-fashioned telegraph. Edison's first job was as telegrapher for Western Union.*

was baffled. Another time he electrified the water dipper. Anyone taking a drink received a shock. People did not always share Edison's sense of humor and they did not appreciate his experiments. He wore out his welcome a few times. Edison did not care. He would pick up and move on to another city.

"I Am Going to Hustle . . ."

Edison took the train to Boston in the winter of 1868. A friend had told him of a job at the Western Union office. He went straight there to apply for the job. Everybody looked up when Edison walked in the door. Some of the workers could not help but stare at the young man. His clothes were crumpled and slept in. His hair needed a comb. He had a slow Midwestern drawl that sounded funny to their ears. The office manager decided to give the scruffy, young man a chance. "You start tonight," he said. When Edison showed up for his shift, he noticed that he was the center of much attention. He was told to take a seat. His first task would be to take down an incoming message from New York. Edison saw at once he was the brunt of a joke. The man in New York started off at a rapid pace that only grew faster. The other men watched to see how he would do. Edison kept pace with him. There were a few minutes of lightning-quick correspondence. Then Edison wired him, "You seem to be tired, suppose you send a little with your other foot."[1] All the men began to laugh with Edison. He might have looked

CHAPTER 3

This illustration appeared in Puck magazine on October 23, 1878. The artist shows how Edison's invention of electric light will put an end to the monopoly that gas companies had on lighting people's homes. Electric light would be much less expensive.

LIGHT THROWN

A DARK SUBJECT.

like a country bumpkin, but he could keep up with the best of them.

BOSTON: THE HEART OF NEW ENGLAND INDUSTRY

Edison had been all over the country. He had worked in Cincinnati and Indianapolis. He had seen Nashville, Memphis, Fort Wayne, and Louisville. Boston was a different kind of city. It was a center of industry. Mills had sprung up all over New England over the last hundred years. Workers at the mill made products like cotton and wool cloth. Boston was at the heart of it all. Machine shops lined the streets, and students came from all over to study at the city's famous schools. There were so many bright, talented people trying to find ways to use science to make a better future. The telegraph was a great new idea. People were making lots of money. What would the future bring? How else could people use electricity? Businessmen were looking for new ideas. They had money to give to inventors with good ideas.

Edison rented a small room in a boarding-house. Many college students rented rooms there, too. Other students worked the night shift at Western Union. Edison liked to talk about science with the students. One day he was in a second-hand bookstore. He picked up a three-volume book about electricity. The book was by a scientist

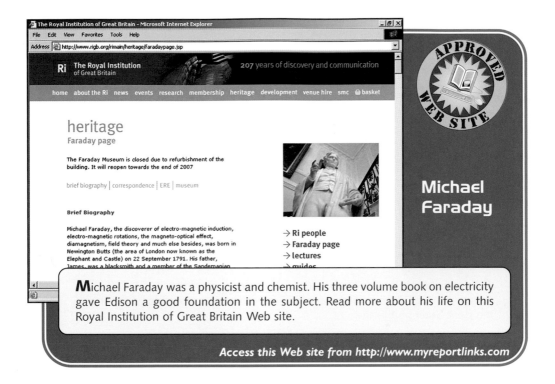

The Royal Institution of Great Britain - Microsoft Internet Explorer

File Edit View Favorites Tools Help

Address http://www.rigb.org/rimain/heritage/faradaypage.jsp

Ri **The Royal Institution** of Great Britain   207 years of discovery and communication

home about the Ri news events research membership heritage development venue hire smc basket

heritage
Faraday page

The Faraday Museum is closed due to refurbishment of the building. It will reopen towards the end of 2007

brief biography | correspondence | ERE | museum

Brief Biography

Michael Faraday, the discoverer of electro-magnetic induction, electro-magnetic rotations, the magneto-optical effect, diamagnetism, field theory and much else besides, was born in Newington Butts (the area of London now known as the Elephant and Castle) on 22 September 1791. His father, James, was a blacksmith and a member of the Sandemanian

→ Ri people
→ Faraday page
→ lectures
→ guides

Michael Faraday

Michael Faraday was a physicist and chemist. His three volume book on electricity gave Edison a good foundation in the subject. Read more about his life on this Royal Institution of Great Britain Web site.

Access this Web site from http://www.myreportlinks.com

named Michael Faraday. He and Edison were a lot alike. Faraday had not gone to college. He had learned what he knew on his own. Edison was excited. He stayed up all night reading. When his roommate awoke in the morning, Edison had still not slept a wink. Edison said to his roommate, "I have got so much to do and life is so short that I am going to hustle." With those words, Edison took off at a run to get his breakfast.[2]

Edison liked to work the night shift. Other night-shift workers slept most of the day, but not Edison. He took short catnaps that left his days free to read and study. He could also tinker. He opened a small workshop where he could experiment. He

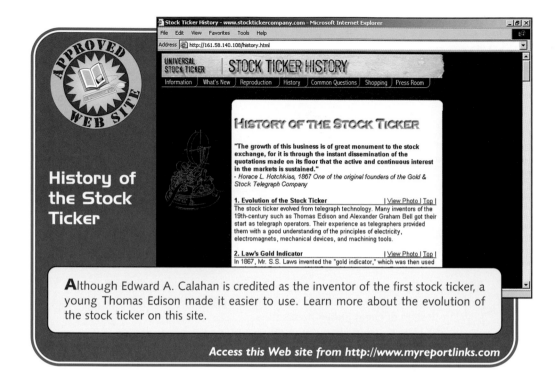

Access this Web site from http://www.myreportlinks.com

spent his paychecks on books, equipment, and chemicals. Then, in 1869, Edison quit his job. He did not like a new rule at work—workers would no longer be allowed to experiment with the company's equipment. That was the last straw for Edison.[3] He decided to take a gamble. He would focus all his time on inventing. He was working on several exciting ideas.

INVENTING TO PAY THE BILLS

By now Edison knew a lot about the telegraph. The telegraph could send only one message at a time. Would it be possible to send more than one? He thought it should be. He invented a telegraph duplex. It could send two telegraphs at the same time along one wire. Edison began to work with a cousin of the telegraph: the stock ticker. A stock ticker was a new machine used on Wall Street. It printed the price of gold on a strip of moving paper. It saved a lot of time in the financial district. Everyone there needed to keep abreast of the price of gold since gold's value was always going up and down. Other markets base the prices of their products on the current price of gold. Edison went to New York and bought some stock tickers. He brought them back to Boston where he opened a store to sell the tickers. Of course Edison soon saw ways to make the stock tickers even better. It was around this time that Edison received his first patent.

⇢ A Lesson Learned

Edison's first patent was for an electric vote recorder. He thought it would be a terrific help to the state legislature. It would replace their roll call system of voting, which took a long time. Here is how the vote recorder worked. Legislators would flick a switch to vote yes or no. This would send an electric current to a piece of paper at the front of the room. The current would react with a chemical. The chemical made a stain in the yes column or no column next to the legislator's name. Then someone just had to look at the paper to know the

Franklin Pope - Microsoft Internet Explorer

File   Edit   View   Favorites   Tools   Help

Address http://www.telegraph-history.org/pope/

Frank L. Pope

Telegraphic and Electrical Engineer

It is not necessary to have a interest in the telegraph to appreciate the life and career of Franklin Pope. It is only necessary to have an interest as to why this one man influenced so many electricians, engineers, and telegraph operators during the 19th century. Why did his writings find their way into the libraries of most of these individuals? Why was his opinion so valued by some of the largest companies in the U.S.?

In researching electrical related technologies in the U.S. during this era, it is common to see a reference to Pope. His career as a telegraph operator, inventor, engineer, writer, explorer, artist, patent attorney, historian, and consultant provided him with a lifetime of experiences necessary to earn the reputation of a true expert. This one time business partner and mentor of a young Thomas Edison emerged telegraph industry to become one of the most respected ele in America. In 1886 he was elected the second president of Th of Electrical Engineers.

Frank Pope was once a business partner of Thomas Edison. Learn more about his life when you visit this **Frank L. Pope** Web page. You will also see a number of Pope's drawings and diagrams of his important inventions.

results of the vote. It took no time at all. Edison knew it would save a lot of time. But there was something he did not know, and that was that no one wanted to save time. Legislators did not want to get rid of the roll call vote. If they did, they would lose an important tool: the filibuster. A filibuster is a way to block a bill and keep it from passing into law. During the roll call vote, the legislators take turns talking. They try to delay the vote on purpose. This buys them time to change people's minds. Edison was let down that no one liked his idea. He learned his lesson from the fiasco. From then on, he vowed to invent useful things that people would buy.[4]

→ Success in New York

Edison had put all of his money into the success of his vote recorder. Now he had no money and no job. Edison took a boat bound for New York City with just a dollar in his pocket. Although he had no job waiting in New York, he was optimistic. He thought he knew how to make an invention people would want. He would make a better stock ticker. He went right to Wall Street, the center of New York's financial district. A friend felt sorry for Edison when he heard he had no place to live and no money. He let Edison sleep in a back room at the Gold and Stock Indicator Company until he found work. Edison had not been there long when a machine ground to a halt. No one knew what to do. Edison calmly asked if he might take a look and he quickly saw the problem. A spring had come loose and fallen into the gears. Edison fixed the machine in no time. The man in charge was very pleased and hired Edison on the spot. He would earn three hundred dollars a month to take care of the equipment.[5] It was more money than Edison was used to. He had only made seventy-five dollars a month when he had worked at Western Union.

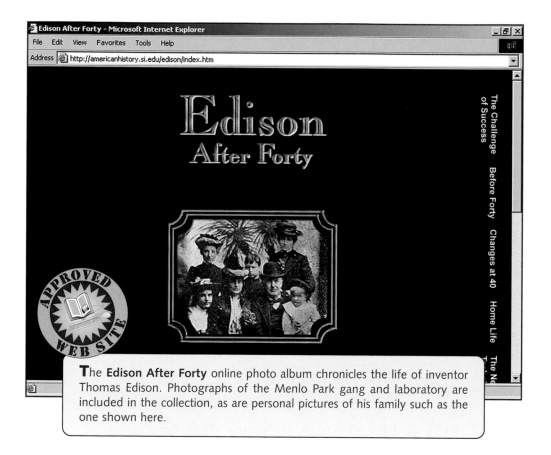

Edison After Forty - Microsoft Internet Explorer

File   Edit   View   Favorites   Tools   Help

Address http://americanhistory.si.edu/edison/index.htm

The Challenge of Success   Before Forty   Changes at 40   Home Life   The Ne

The **Edison After Forty** online photo album chronicles the life of inventor Thomas Edison. Photographs of the Menlo Park gang and laboratory are included in the collection, as are personal pictures of his family such as the one shown here.

With his new income, Edison set up a shop for inventing in his off hours. Working with another man named Franklin Pope, Edison soon patented a greatly improved stock ticker. The Gold Company bought the new stock ticker. The price was forty thousand dollars. Edison was twenty-three years old and he had just made a small fortune. It looked like inventing might pay the bills after all. What did Edison do with all that money? He bought a building in Newark, New Jersey, set up a factory, and hired three hundred people. They would make Edison's new stock tickers and sell them to the Gold Company. Edison was still thinking about the telegraph, too. He knew there were ways to make it better. He had an idea for a quadruplex. The quadruplex would handle four messages at a time. It could send two messages along a wire. At the same time, two messages could travel in the other direction.

A Christmas Wedding

Edison's career was off to a wonderful start. Now all he wanted was a wife to share his happiness.

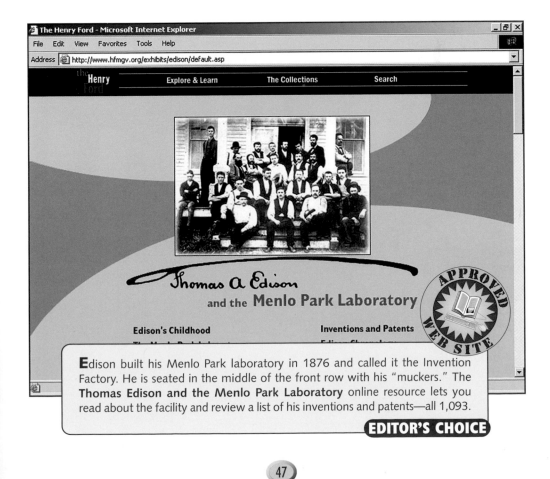

The Henry Ford - Microsoft Internet Explorer

File   Edit   View   Favorites   Tools   Help

Address http://www.hfmgv.org/exhibits/edison/default.asp

the Henry Ford

Explore & Learn   The Collections   Search

Thomas A. Edison
and the **Menlo Park Laboratory**

APPROVED WEB SITE

Edison's Childhood

Inventions and Patents

Edison built his Menlo Park laboratory in 1876 and called it the Invention Factory. He is seated in the middle of the front row with his "muckers." The **Thomas Edison and the Menlo Park Laboratory** online resource lets you read about the facility and review a list of his inventions and patents—all 1,093.

EDITOR'S CHOICE

In this photo, Edison is seated in the center, surrounded by some of his workers at his Orange laboratory. Charles Batchelor is standing second from the left. Batchelor was a long-time Edison worker who also worked at the Menlo Park facility.

One of the workers in his Newark factory caught his eye. With long blond hair and bright eyes, Mary Stilwell was a beauty. Like Edison, Mary came from the middle class, and she had not gone to school for long. Edison was very shy at first. He was twenty-four. Mary was just sixteen. Once he got up the courage to talk to Mary, he swept her off her feet. Within three months, the two were married. They married on Christmas Day, 1871.

STARTING A FAMILY

The young couple went on a honeymoon. They spent all of their time together. Once they were home, it was a different story. Edison went right back to his old work habits. He threw his all into solving problems. He would not rest until he had answers. He would even eat and sleep at the laboratory. Mary did not understand. Why did her husband stop spending time with her? She wished it could be as it had when they were courting.[6] She came from a big family and was not used to being home all alone. Mary tried to make herself feel better. She bought expensive food and beautiful new clothes. Nothing worked. She grew anxious and was often sick.[7] The Edisons eventually had three children over the next five years. Their names were Marion, Thomas Alva, Jr., and William. Their father had fond nicknames for them. Marion was "Dot" and

Thomas was "Dash," after the dots and dashes that made up Morse code.

THE INVENTION FACTORY AT MENLO PARK

Edison needed a change. He was tired of working in his Newark shop. It was a factory, not a laboratory. There were hundreds of people busy at work. It was too busy for Edison. He wanted a quiet place where he could think up new ideas. So, in 1875, Edison moved with his family to Menlo Park, New Jersey. Menlo Park was 12 miles (19 kilometers) south of crowded Newark. The small town seemed a world away. His laboratory at Menlo Park was built to meet his needs. There was a library filled with science books. The machine shop could make anything that Edison could dream up. The chemical store room contained thousands of substances. There were electric batteries and a steam engine. Edison had come a long way since the days of the bottles marked "POISON" in his parent's cellar. His laboratory was one of a kind. No one else in the United States had this kind of resource at their disposal.

Edison stocked his lab with talented men. Charles Batchelor was Edison's right-hand man. He was an expert with machines. Batchelor was British. He came to America to work in the mills. After Edison came up with an idea, he handed it over to John Kruesi in the machine shop, and Kruesi

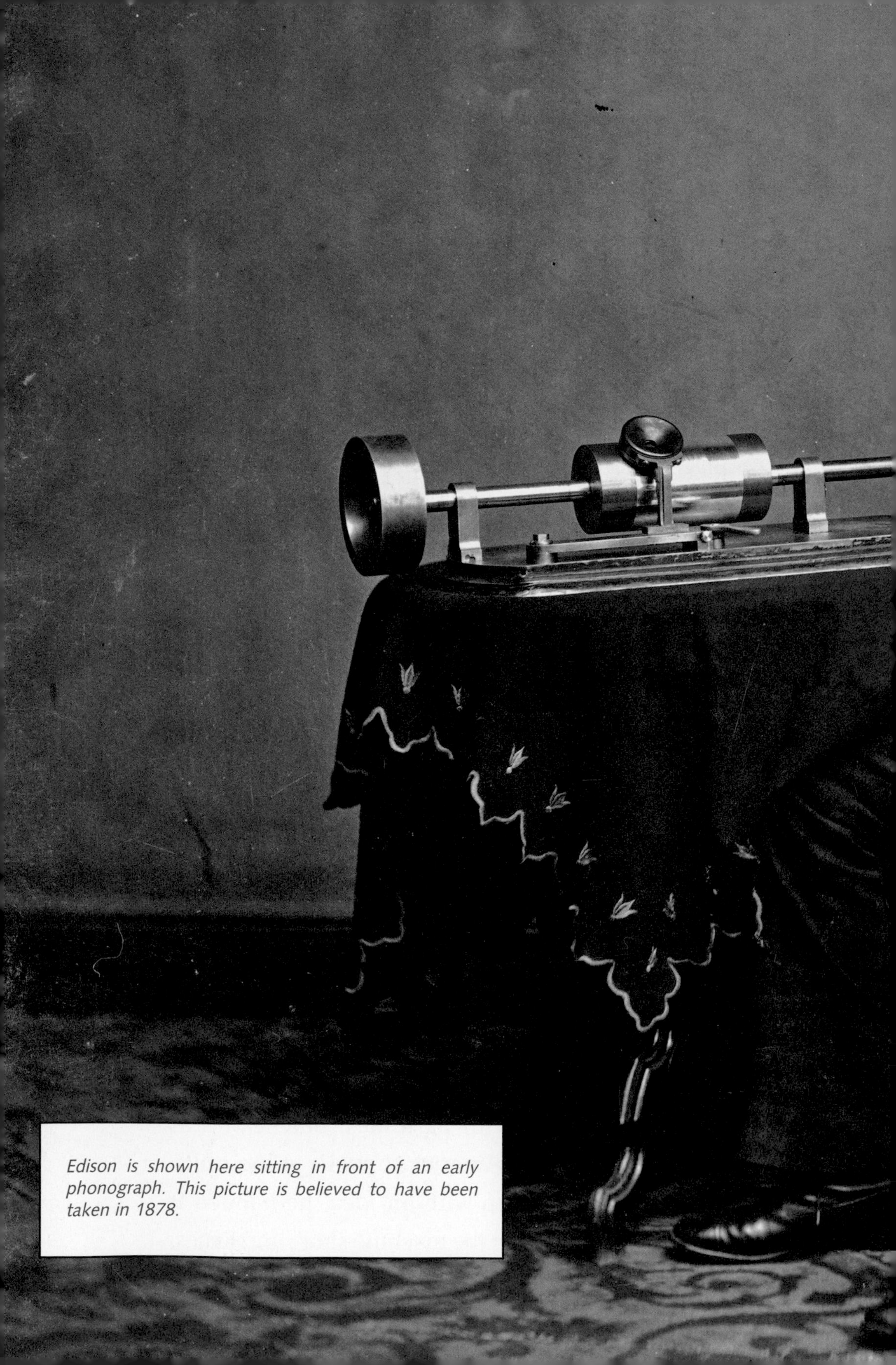

Edison is shown here sitting in front of an early phonograph. This picture is believed to have been taken in 1878.

would build a model. Kruesi had trained as a machinist in Swiss clock shops, where men were famous for their precise work. John Ott was another machinist who came to Menlo Park from the Newark shop. The team of men worked well together. They would test an invention and try again and again until they got it right. Edison called his workers the "muckers," and he was the Chief Mucker. His workers affectionately called him the Old Man. He was just thirty years old, but his hair had already gone white.

⊜ Doing Things Differently

Menlo Park was a kind of factory. Inventions were the products they made there. Business leaders did not like it. Edison was a scientist who made things to sell. Making and selling things was their business. Edison worked outside their control. If only Edison would go to work for them. Scientists did not like it either. Science was pure. It should be studied for the sake of understanding the world. It was in bad taste to study science only to make products to sell.[8] Edison saw it in a different light. He loved to experiment. He was also driven to solve problems. It was true that he wanted to make money. He needed money so that he could do more inventing. He wanted nothing more than the freedom to follow his many ideas to see if they would work.

⇒ THE INSOMNIA SQUAD

When there was a problem to solve, Edison was known to lock the doors to the lab. No one was allowed to leave until he had succeeded. This must have made him difficult to work for sometimes. His high energy and enthusiasm were catching. One worker even claimed he would have paid Edison for the honor of working at Menlo Park.[9] His workers formed a close-knit team and dubbed themselves the Insomnia Squad. Like Edison, they stayed up all hours of the night. The team would often take a midnight break. They bought some food from a nearby farm. After wolfing down a late night meal, they would sing, joke, and tell stories. Then they would return to work before heading home to catch a few hours sleep.

"INVENTION IS ONE PERCENT INSPIRATION AND 99% PERSPIRATION"

Alexander Graham Bell made the world's first telephone in 1876. People called it the "talking telegraph" at first. It was a lot like a telegraph. The telegraph sent the sound of dots and dashes along a wire. The telephone also sent sounds along a wire. It sent the sound made by a person's voice. Edison thought Bell had a good idea. He was also sure he could make an even better telephone. He set to work on it. While he worked on the telephone, he came across something amazing. It was something no one had ever done before. He found a way to record and replay his voice. Edison came up with a name for his new invention—the phonograph. He took it to Washington, D.C., and showed it to Congress and President Rutherford B. Hayes. Everyone was awestruck by the talking machine. Edison and his phonograph were the talk of the town. Now there was never a moment of peace at Menlo Park. Edison was proud of his work and was happy to show it off. Still, he soon grew tired of being in the spotlight. He longed for some peace and quiet. He had so many new ideas he wanted to explore.

CHAPTER

4

For two months in the summer of 1878, Edison took a break. He left New Jersey and his work behind. He rode by train to the American West. He hunted, fished, and camped out under the stars. All the while he thought about inventing. In July, he met up with many other scientists from all over the globe. They all came to the town of Rawlins, Wyoming, to watch a solar eclipse. During a solar eclipse, the moon comes between the earth and the sun. For a few minutes, the sky grows as dark as night. It was a spectacular thing to see and made Edison feel better. When he returned to Menlo Park, he was his old, energetic self again. He had a new challenge in mind. He was going to find a way to use electricity to make light. Edison was going to light up people's homes.

➡ THE HISTORY OF ELECTRIC LIGHTING

When you hear the name Edison, you probably think of the lightbulb. It is his most famous invention. Yet Edison was not the first person to make a lightbulb. He did, however, make the first one that worked well. Other scientists in the United States and in Europe were working on the same lines. It was a race to see who would solve the problem first. Edison had something the rest

The Ediphone, an improvement over Bell's original telephone was one of Edison's most useful creations. Here, he receives a flag from Ediphone Distributors to honor him on the forty-third anniversary of the Ediphone invention.

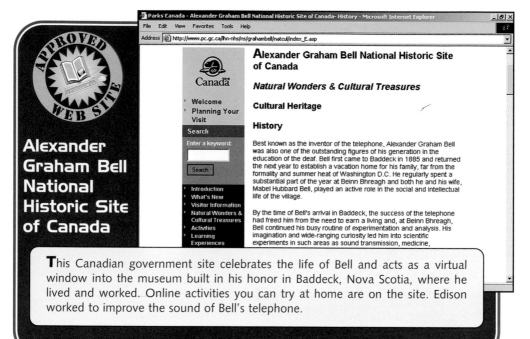

Parks Canada - Alexander Graham Bell National Historic Site of Canada- History - Microsoft Internet Explorer

File   Edit   View   Favorites   Tools   Help

Address http://www.pc.gc.ca/lhn-nhs/ns/grahambell/natcul/index_E.asp

Canada

Welcome
Planning Your
Visit

Search

Enter a keyword:

Search

Introduction
What's New
Visitor Information
Natural Wonders &
Cultural Treasures
Activities
Learning
Experiences

Alexander Graham Bell National Historic Site of Canada

Natural Wonders & Cultural Treasures

Cultural Heritage

History

Best known as the inventor of the telephone, Alexander Graham Bell was also one of the outstanding figures of his generation in the education of the deaf. Bell first came to Baddeck in 1885 and returned the next year to establish a vacation home for his family, far from the formality and summer heat of Washington D.C. He regularly spent a substantial part of the year at Beinn Bhreagh and both he and his wife, Mabel Hubbard Bell, played an active role in the social and intellectual life of the village.

By the time of Bell's arrival in Baddeck, the success of the telephone had freed him from the need to earn a living and, at Beinn Bhreagh, Bell continued his busy routine of experimentation and analysis. His imagination and wide-ranging curiosity led him into scientific experiments in such areas as sound transmission, medicine,

Alexander Graham Bell National Historic Site of Canada

This Canadian government site celebrates the life of Bell and acts as a virtual window into the museum built in his honor in Baddeck, Nova Scotia, where he lived and worked. Online activities you can try at home are on the site. Edison worked to improve the sound of Bell's telephone.

Access this Web site from http://www.myreportlinks.com

of the pack did not. He had access to plenty of money. People were lining up to invest their money in Edison's next venture. They believed in Edison. If he said he would make electric light, no doubt he would do it. In September, Edison gave an interview with the *New York Sun*. He said he would have an electric light in a matter of weeks.[1] By October, people could buy stock in the Edison Electric Light Company. It had the support of America's wealthiest men. Now Edison just had to invent the product!

People had found a way to use electric lights outdoors. They were called arc lamps. Some cities lit their streets with arc lamps. In an arc lamp, the electricity jumped between two carbon rods. It produced a blinding spark of light. The lamps were not for indoor use. The bright glare would hurt people's eyes. Plus, as the carbon burned up, the lamps released toxic fumes. It took a lot of energy to power the lamps. Edison felt the arc lamp was not the answer. It was too powerful. The solution, he believed, was to subdivide the bright electric light into many smaller lamps. One source would provide power for many lamps.

People had tried to make electric lights that would work indoors. Scientists had experimented with incandescent light since 1838.[2] Incandescent means something is so hot that it glows. They had put an electric current through a variety of substances. Slowly they heated the substances until they glowed. Yet they all soon melted or caught fire. A fire needs oxygen to burn. Oxygen is a gas that is found in the air. So the scientists tried again—this time inside a vacuum. A vacuum is a space that has nothing in it, not even air. To make a vacuum, scientists pumped out the air from a glass bulb. Now the substances would glow longer. No one had made a lightbulb that would work for more than a few hours. No one, that is, until Edison.

⊜ A GRAND VISION

Edison had a grand vision for the future. He was not just trying to make a working lightbulb. He

This old lightbulb is very much like some of the first ones that Edison invented.

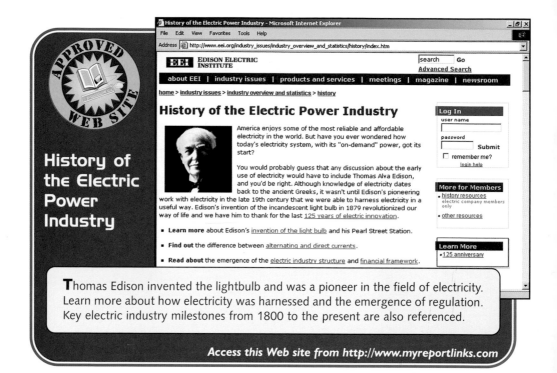

History of the Electric Power Industry - Microsoft Internet Explorer

File   Edit   View   Favorites   Tools   Help

Address   http://www.eei.org/industry_issues/industry_overview_and_statistics/history/index.htm

EDISON ELECTRIC
INSTITUTE   search   Go
                                                         Advanced Search

about EEI | industry issues | products and services | meetings | magazine | newsroom

home > industry issues > industry overview and statistics > history

History of the Electric Power Industry

America enjoys some of the most reliable and affordable electricity in the world. But have you ever wondered how today's electricity system, with its "on-demand" power, got its start?

You would probably guess that any discussion about the early use of electricity would have to include Thomas Alva Edison, and you'd be right. Although knowledge of electricity dates back to the ancient Greeks, it wasn't until Edison's pioneering work with electricity in the late 19th century that we were able to harness electricity in a useful way. Edison's invention of the incandescent light bulb in 1879 revolutionized our way of life and we have him to thank for the last 125 years of electric innovation.

- **Learn more** about Edison's invention of the light bulb and his Pearl Street Station.

- **Find out** the difference between alternating and direct currents.

- **Read about** the emergence of the electric industry structure and financial framework.

Log In
user name

password
                    Submit
☐ remember me?
        login help

More for Members
• history resources
  electric company members only
• other resources

Learn More
• 125 anniversary

Thomas Edison invented the lightbulb and was a pioneer in the field of electricity. Learn more about how electricity was harnessed and the emergence of regulation. Key electric industry milestones from 1800 to the present are also referenced.

Access this Web site from http://www.myreportlinks.com

wanted to create a whole electrical system. He dreamed of lighting up New York City with electric indoor lights. There would need to be a central power station, he thought. That is where the electricity would be made. The power station would have machines called generators that would use steam power to make electricity. The electricity could run through insulated wires and the wires would run under the streets, just like the gas pipes. Electric lights would be cheap, he believed. They would cost a fraction of the price of gas lights. He knew it would work. It was just a matter of figuring out how. The way to make indoor electric lights evaded him. Weeks went by. There was no news from Menlo Park. Weeks turned into months. People began to have doubts. Maybe Edison could not do it after all. Many scientists of the day stated it was flatout impossible to light a home or building by electricity.

⮕ UPTON JOINS THE TEAM

Edison made no secret that he disliked math. He thought math got in the way of his creative inventing style. Edison liked to try out an idea. If it did not work, he would throw it out and try something else. He did not mind trying things over and over again. Eventually he was sure to hit on success. The electric light had so many new factors. Edison was doing thousands of tests and each time he learned a little more. The tests were also taking a lot of time. If only he understood math better, he could narrow down the possibilities on a piece of paper. He needed help from someone who knew a lot about math. So he hired a bright mathematician from Princeton University. Francis Upton was quite the opposite of Edison. Upton was at home in the classroom. He dressed in tidy clothes. Edison usually wore a dirty lab coat. He was at ease in the machine shop. Even though Edison did not think much of math, he had a lot of respect for Upton.[3] With Upton on board, the experiments grew more productive.

⊛ THE SEARCH FOR THE PERFECT "BURNER"

What would be the best substance to use in his lightbulb? Edison needed something that would glow, not burn or melt. He called this material the "burner." He wanted something thin and long, like a wire or thread.[4] He tried the metal platinum. It seemed like a good idea since it can get very hot and still not melt. Edison solved a major piece of the puzzle when he realized platinum was no good. It did not resist the electric current; the current was able to pass right through. It took a lot of electricity to get the metal to glow. The right substance, he saw, would offer a lot of resistance to the electric current. Then he would not need to use as much electricity. When the current met with resistance, the pressure created friction, a kind of energy. This energy would help to heat the filament.[5] But what could he use that would have the right resistance? He knew that carbon did not let a current pass easily through it. Carbon burns quickly in the air, but not in a vacuum.

The Menlo Park team worked at full throttle. They tried carbon in many shapes and sizes. The pressure was on. It had now been a year since Edison began work on the electric light. What was taking so long? And then, on October 21, 1879, Edison made a lightbulb that worked. He and his workers watched as their latest lightbulb continued to glow for a whole day. They took turns

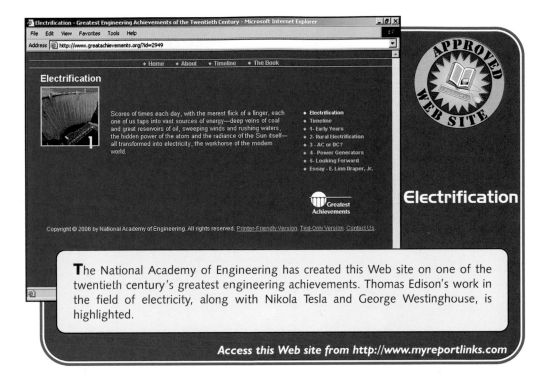

Electrification - Greatest Engineering Achievements of the Twentieth Century - Microsoft Internet Explorer

File   Edit   View   Favorites   Tools   Help

Address http://www.greatachievements.org/?id=2949

◆ Home   ◆ About   ◆ Timeline   ◆ The Book

Electrification

Scores of times each day, with the merest flick of a finger, each one of us taps into vast sources of energy—deep veins of coal and great reservoirs of oil, sweeping winds and rushing waters, the hidden power of the atom and the radiance of the Sun itself—all transformed into electricity, the workhorse of the modern world.

◆ Electrification
◆ Timeline
◆ 1- Early Years
◆ 2- Rural Electrification
◆ 3 - AC or DC?
◆ 4 - Power Generators
◆ 5- Looking Forward
◆ Essay - E. Linn Draper, Jr.

Greatest Achievements

Electrification

Copyright © 2006 by National Academy of Engineering. All rights reserved. Printer-Friendly Version. Text-Only Version. Contact Us.

The National Academy of Engineering has created this Web site on one of the twentieth century's greatest engineering achievements. Thomas Edison's work in the field of electricity, along with Nikola Tesla and George Westinghouse, is highlighted.

Access this Web site from http://www.myreportlinks.com

watching in shifts. The bulb stayed lit for over forty-five hours. It had a carbon filament made from a cotton sewing thread. Edison was elated, but the work was far from over. They knew carbon would work. Now the search was on for a good source of carbon. They tried everything they could put their hands on. They used cardboard, paper, wood, coconut shell, and fishing line. Edison even tried making a filter from a piece of a bamboo fan. His creativity paid off. The bamboo burned well. Now Edison wanted to find the best kind of bamboo. He sent men on a worldwide hunt for bamboo. The world was his stockroom. The public read about the inventor's latest search

▲ This 1914 photo shows Edison walking (center) with Miller Reese Hutchinson on his left and fellow inventor Lewis Miller on his right. Edison married Lewis Miller's daughter, Mina.

in the newspapers, and people followed the story with great interest.[6]

Pearl Street Station

Now that the lamps worked, Edison put them on display. He threw a New Year's Eve party at Menlo Park. Seven hundred lamps lit up over one square mile (2.6 square kilometers).[7] People were impressed by this new light without a flame. Some people could afford to buy electric lights right away. J. P. Morgan was one of the richest men in the United States, and he had his home wired for electric light. He thought the lights were great, but his neighbors did not agree. They complained that the generator was much too noisy.[8] Edison wanted to see his lights everywhere, not just in the homes of rich men. He set to work on building the world's first power station.

He bought two buildings on Pearl Street in lower Manhattan where he would make enough power to light up the city. Steam engines would make energy. Twelve generators would turn the energy into electricity. Workmen put down cables under the streets. Wires threaded through the cables that would deliver the electricity to homes and businesses. Edison left Menlo Park and moved back into New York City to oversee the work. No one had ever tried to do this before. Edison had to make it up as he went along. He designed the

John Pierpont Morgan, Jr.,
better known as J. P. Morgan,
was a giant of the banking
industry and one of the
wealthiest men in the world.

Guide to the Mina Miller Edison Collection - Microsoft Internet Explorer

File   Edit   View   Favorites   Tools   Help

Address   http://www.ciweb.org/mina_miller.html

Guide to the Mina Miller Edison Collection

Done

Mina Miller Edison was the daughter of Chautauqua cofounder Lewis Miller and the second wife of Thomas Edison. The Web site for the **Mina Miller Edison Collection** contains a biographical sketch and a chronology of her life.

switches, fuses, and outlets. He even made the meters to measure how much electricity each home used. In 1882 the station was complete, and the world never looked back. Within ten years, there were hundreds of other cities around the world with Edison-style power plants.

⇒ Tragedy Strikes

In the middle of all this success, Edison's wife, Mary, passed away. Her doctor said the cause of death was brain fever. She was only twenty-nine years old. In those days, raising the children was the

▲ A photoprint of Mina Edison, taken around 1906.

wife's duty. That had been Mary's job. Now Edison spent more time with his children. His daughter Marion hardly left his side. Edison's eyes opened up to the world outside of work. For the only time in his life, he wrote his thoughts down in a personal diary. A year passed. Edison spent the summer with friends on the coast of Massachusetts. His friends planned to find a suitable new wife for the busy inventor. They introduced him to Mina Miller. Mina was smart, young, and beautiful. Her father was a wealthy inventor from Ohio. Edison taught Mina the dots and dashes of telegraphy. They tapped silent messages onto the backs of each other's hands. To Mina's great surprise, Edison tapped out "Will you marry me?" She replied, "Yes." The two were married on February 24, 1886. They bought a grand new home, Glenmont, in the exclusive neighborhood of Llewellyn Park, New Jersey. Mina and Edison would have three children together: Madeleine, Charles, and Theodore.

⇒ WIZARD RELOCATES TO WEST ORANGE

Edison built a workplace closer to his new home. Now he was the wizard of West Orange, New Jersey. The facility was ten times the size of Menlo Park. The imposing brick buildings really did look like a factory. There were offices, machine shops, a library, stockrooms, and a music room. There was even a dark room for photography. Edison

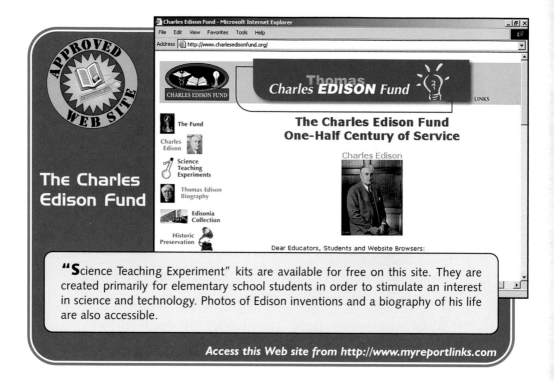

The Charles
Edison Fund

Charles Edison Fund - Microsoft Internet Explorer

File   Edit   View   Favorites   Tools   Help

Address http://www.charlesedisonfund.org/

CHARLES EDISON FUND

Thomas
Charles **EDISON** Fund

LINKS

The Fund

Charles
Edison

Science
Teaching
Experiments

Thomas Edison
Biography

Edisonia
Collection

Historic
Preservation

The Charles Edison Fund
One-Half Century of Service

Charles Edison

Dear Educators, Students and Website Browsers:

"Science Teaching Experiment" kits are available for free on this site. They are created primarily for elementary school students in order to stimulate an interest in science and technology. Photos of Edison inventions and a biography of his life are also accessible.

Access this Web site from http://www.myreportlinks.com

even hired guards to make sure only the workers could enter. The Menlo Park days were over. Never again would Edison enjoy the incredible inspiration that he found as a young man with a small team of men to help him.[9] That is not to say his inventing days were over. That would be far from the truth. Edison never stopped looking for ways to make the world better.

INVENTING THINGS THAT WOULD SELL

You could say Edison was at the right place at the right time. He came of age at a time when humans were just starting to learn about electricity. It was a brand new source of energy. People knew it could help them, but how? Edison looked for answers to that question. He led the world in finding ways to use this new energy. He came up with many ideas to make people's lives easier. He invented so many things that it is impossible to do them all justice here. These are some of most important things Edison made. Even though Edison the man is long gone, his machines continue to help us. They still shape the world we know today.

CHAPTER 5

➔ A MICROPHONE FOR THE TELEPHONE

Alexander Graham Bell owned the idea for the telephone. He had a patent to prove it. A patent is a legal piece of paper, and the holder of a patent owns the rights to the invention. What would happen if an inventor did not have a patent? Anyone could come along and take the idea. A patent only lasts for a set period of time. It does not stop other people from trying to build on the idea and

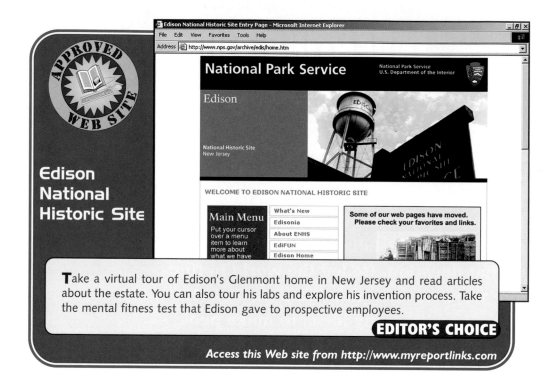

Edison National Historic Site

National Park Service

National Park Service
U.S. Department of the Interior

Edison

National Historic Site
New Jersey

WELCOME TO EDISON NATIONAL HISTORIC SITE

Main Menu

Put your cursor over a menu item to learn more about what we have

What's New

Edisonia

About ENHS

EdiFUN

Edison Home

Some of our web pages have moved.
Please check your favorites and links.

Take a virtual tour of Edison's Glenmont home in New Jersey and read articles about the estate. You can also tour his labs and explore his invention process. Take the mental fitness test that Edison gave to prospective employees.

EDITOR'S CHOICE

Access this Web site from http://www.myreportlinks.com

make it better. In fact, Edison often did just this. The first telephone had some problems. It did not work well over long distances. There was only one part for talking and listening. A person spoke into it, and then quickly held it up to his ear to hear the reply. The sound was muffled. It needed to be fixed before it could be a useful tool. Even though it had some issues, the telephone was a threat to the telegraph empire. Western Union hired Edison and asked him to take Bell's basic idea and improve on it.[1]

Now Edison was quite hard of hearing. He could not hear the faint sounds of a voice through Bell's telephone. The sound was faint even to a normal ear. How in the world would Edison do experiments with sounds he could not hear? Where there is a will, there is a way. Edison held a metal plate in his mouth. Wires attached the plate to the phone's sound piece. He could feel the sound vibrations through the sensitive nerve endings in his teeth.[2] Bell's telephone had a thin piece of metal inside the mouthpiece. When a person spoke into it, the sound waves of the voice made the metal vibrate. The telephone changed the waves of sound into electric impulses. It sent the impulses through a wire. Edison saw the problem: the voice's sound waves were not strong enough. They could not make clear enough impulses, not

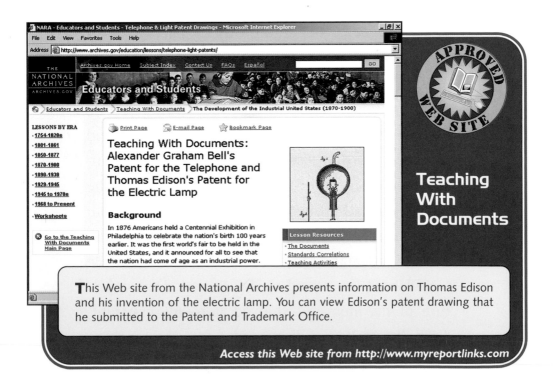

This Web site from the National Archives presents information on Thomas Edison and his invention of the electric lamp. You can view Edison's patent drawing that he submitted to the Patent and Trademark Office.

Access this Web site from http://www.myreportlinks.com

on their own. What if they had help? Edison came up with a new design. He used carbon from lampblack. Lampblack is the soot that forms when a kerosene lamp burns. The sound waves of the voice now moved two carbon buttons. The carbon allowed for a much stronger electric signal. The volume and clarity of the voice improved. It also made it possible for the phone to work over longer distances. The same kind of microphone is used in telephones even now.

THE PHONOGRAPH: A TALKING MACHINE

Now that the telephone worked well, what else needed to happen? Well, the telephone was a lot like the telegraph. Edison thought about what happened at a telegraph office. The operator wrote down each message. A record was kept of all the telegraphs. Maybe people would want a record of telephone messages, too.[3] How could he make a record of the sound waves? He conceived of a machine that just might work. It was a cylinder covered in tinfoil. A needle would record the sound waves by making a groove in the tinfoil. Then a second needle would move over the groove and make the same sound waves. People would hear the sound again. Edison drew a picture of his idea and showed it to his assistant, John Kruesi. Kruesi disappeared into the machine shop. When he came back out, he held the first

Edison as an older man, seated in front of a phonograph.

model of the phonograph. Edison gave it a try. He recited the first thing that came to his mind: "Mary Had a Little Lamb." When he cranked the machine again, it replayed his voice. The men whooped and hollered and patted Edison on the back. It had worked on the first try.

The phonograph was a brand-new idea. No one else had come close to recording sound. People did not think it could be done. So when Edison found a way, people were eager to see what the fuss was about. Hotels had phonographs in their lobbies. To hear a song, a person had to put a nickel in a slot. Everyone agreed it was amazing. No one was quite sure what the phonograph would be used for. Edison guessed it would be most useful in the business world. One of the first things he tried to market was a talking doll. Stores quickly sold out of the popular new toy. Yet the customers soon returned the dolls to the stores. They complained that the dolls did not work. The talking mechanism was fragile. It ended up that people really wanted to listen to music in their own homes. Edison started a new company to make and sell musical recordings.

THE KINETOSCOPE: A MOVIE CAMERA

Eadweard Muybridge came to see Edison in West Orange in 1888. Muybridge had taken many pictures of a horse while it galloped. He showed the pictures very quickly and in the order they were taken. The horse appeared to be moving. Still, the jerky movement did not look quite real. The photographs did not move fast enough to trick the human eye. The idea of a moving picture intrigued Edison. Maybe he could "do for the eye what the phonograph does for the ear."[4] Edison had the idea of a moving picture with sound— what we today call a movie. He had the idea to take many photographs in a row onto a long strip of film. The film was wound onto a roll. When the film was projected, the images flowed by rapidly. The movement looked smooth and very real.

⊜ THE FIRST MOVIE MACHINE

Today, movies are a huge industry. They bring in billions of dollars each year. It is funny to think they were just a sideline for Edison. Instead, he was busy at his iron mine. He had invested a lot of time and money in the mine. He knew there was no more high-grade iron left in the United States. So Edison had found a way to use low-grade iron. The mine had huge machines that could crush large rocks into powder. The machines were giant but delicate—they often broke down. Edison spent a lot of time at the mine. He put William K. L. Dickson in charge of the moving-picture project. Dickson was a skilled photographer. By 1892, they had made a machine that showed short movies.

EDISON'S

The Metropolitan Print Company created this advertisement for Thomas Edison's vitascope around 1896. The vitascope was a film projector developed by Edison and C. Francis Jenkins.

THE VITASC

GREATEST
MARVEL

OPE

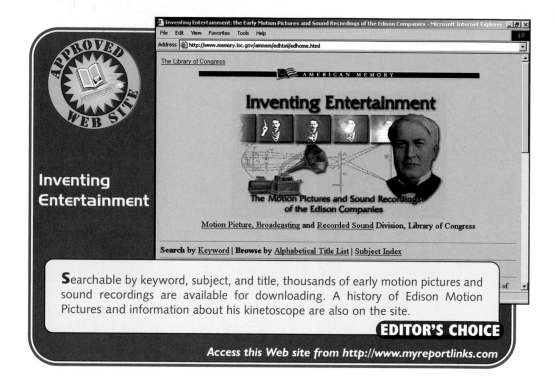

Inventing Entertainment

Inventing Entertainment: the Early Motion Pictures and Sound Recordings of the Edison Companies - Microsoft Internet Explorer

File   Edit   View   Favorites   Tools   Help

Address   http://www.memory.loc.gov/ammem/edhtml/edhome.html

The Library of Congress

AMERICAN MEMORY

Inventing Entertainment

The Motion Pictures and Sound Recordings of the Edison Companies

Motion Picture, Broadcasting and Recorded Sound Division, Library of Congress

Search by Keyword | Browse by Alphabetical Title List | Subject Index

Searchable by keyword, subject, and title, thousands of early motion pictures and sound recordings are available for downloading. A history of Edison Motion Pictures and information about his kinetoscope are also on the site.

EDITOR'S CHOICE

Access this Web site from http://www.myreportlinks.com

They called it the peephole kinetoscope. It looked like a cabinet with a hole in the top. A person looked down in through the hole. Inside the dark box was a tiny image. The show only lasted a few seconds. The idea of a photograph was still a fairly new one. A moving photograph must have seemed quite magical to those first viewers. Now there were slot machine kinetoscopes. The price had gone up though—it was now a quarter. At that time a quarter was a considerable amount, but people did not balk at the price. They stood in long lines to take a turn seeing the latest of Edison's fantastic inventions. The kinetoscope was the new rage.

Edison saw there was a future in motion pictures. He began to make motion pictures that could be shown on a big screen. Now many people could view the picture at the same time. He built the world's first motion picture studio in 1893. The odd shaped building was funny to look at. They had covered it with black tar paper. They painted the inside black, too. The men at the laboratory nicknamed it the Black Maria. The entire building was mounted on a movable base. They did not use artificial lights like they do today. Instead, the building turned to follow the path of the sun. They could raise a portion of the roof to allow light in. Since the first movies were so short, they did not have time to tell a story. One early movie showed two boxers sparring in a ring. Others pictured an organ grinder with a monkey and bears dancing. *A Kiss from the Widow Jones* even showed a man kissing a woman. This was considered a bit risqué.[5] *The Great Train Robbery* (1903) was the first film with a developed plot. With its cops and robbers theme and action-packed chase scene, it set the standard for action films of the future.

THE DANGERS OF ELECTRIC CURRENT: THE ELECTRIC CHAIR

In those days, criminals who were sentenced to die were hanged. The hangings took place in public and were grisly events. Many people did not

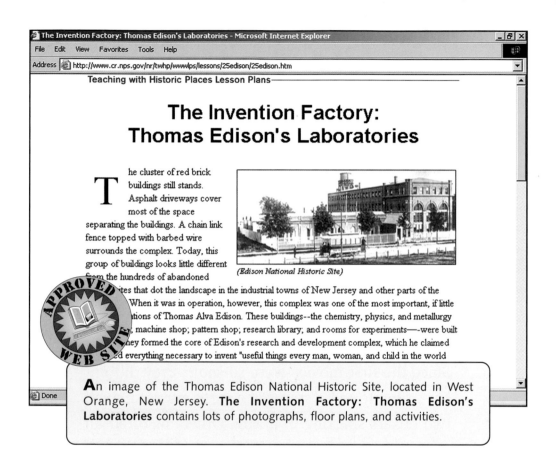

The Invention Factory: Thomas Edison's Laboratories - Microsoft Internet Explorer

File   Edit   View   Favorites   Tools   Help

Address http://www.cr.nps.gov/nr/twhp/wwwlps/lessons/25edison/25edison.htm

Teaching with Historic Places Lesson Plans

The Invention Factory:
Thomas Edison's Laboratories

The cluster of red brick buildings still stands. Asphalt driveways cover most of the space separating the buildings. A chain link fence topped with barbed wire surrounds the complex. Today, this group of buildings looks little different from the hundreds of abandoned

(Edison National Historic Site)

sites that dot the landscape in the industrial towns of New Jersey and other parts of the ...When it was in operation, however, this complex was one of the most important, if little ...tions of Thomas Alva Edison. These buildings--the chemistry, physics, and metallurgy ..., machine shop; pattern shop; research library; and rooms for experiments—-were built ...hey formed the core of Edison's research and development complex, which he claimed ...d everything necessary to invent "useful things every man, woman, and child in the world

An image of the Thomas Edison National Historic Site, located in West Orange, New Jersey. **The Invention Factory: Thomas Edison's Laboratories** contains lots of photographs, floor plans, and activities.

think hanging was the right thing to do. Surely, with all the advances in science, there was a better way. Some people said a strong electric current could kill a person without pain. In 1889, the state of New York took a stand. From now on, they would use an electric current to put their criminals to death. Edison did not think it was a good idea. He did not believe it was right to kill, even as a punishment. It is perhaps a bit odd, then, that he helped to invent the electric chair. At his West Orange laboratory, the experimenters did many gruesome tests. They killed dogs, cows, and even horses with an electric current.[6] They were finding out the fastest way to put a person to death. Edison felt it was his duty to make the process as painless as it could be.[7] But there was another reason, too, and it was not as lofty.

Edison's power stations used a type of electric current called DC. DC stands for direct current. George Westinghouse had started putting up power stations, too. His used an alternating current or AC. AC cost less money. It was just a matter of time before AC won out. Edison was not about to give up without a fight. Edison told people that AC was dangerous, even though it was not true. He tried to link AC with the electric chair. If people knew AC could kill someone, maybe they would be too scared to use it.[8] Edison's plan did not work. AC, which is very safe, is what we use today.

STORAGE BATTERY FOR ELECTRIC CARS

The first automobiles cost too much money for most people. They ran on gasoline, had noisy motors, and gave off smelly fumes. Edison believed he could make a cheap electric car. First he needed to make a better battery. The batteries of the day were not very sturdy. If they bounced around on rough roads, they would break. They were also much too heavy. Plus they had to be recharged a lot. Edison worked on his battery for

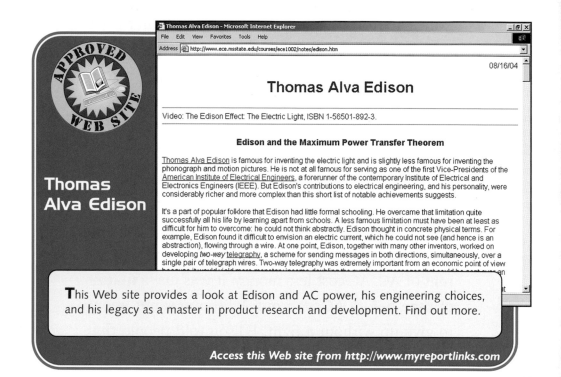

Thomas Alva Edison - Microsoft Internet Explorer

File   Edit   View   Favorites   Tools   Help

Address   http://www.ece.msstate.edu/courses/ece1002/notes/edison.htm

08/16/04

Thomas Alva Edison

Video: The Edison Effect: The Electric Light, ISBN 1-56501-892-3.

Edison and the Maximum Power Transfer Theorem

Thomas Alva Edison is famous for inventing the electric light and is slightly less famous for inventing the phonograph and motion pictures. He is not at all famous for serving as one of the first Vice-Presidents of the American Institute of Electrical Engineers, a forerunner of the contemporary Institute of Electrical and Electronics Engineers (IEEE). But Edison's contributions to electrical engineering, and his personality, were considerably richer and more complex than this short list of notable achievements suggests.

It's a part of popular folklore that Edison had little formal schooling. He overcame that limitation quite successfully all his life by learning apart from schools. A less famous limitation must have been at least as difficult for him to overcome: he could not think abstractly. Edison thought in concrete physical terms. For example, Edison found it difficult to envision an electric current, which he could not see (and hence is an abstraction), flowing through a wire. At one point, Edison, together with many other inventors, worked on developing *two-way* telegraphy, a scheme for sending messages in both directions, simultaneously, over a single pair of telegraph wires. Two-way telegraphy was extremely important from an economic point of view

Thomas Alva Edison

This Web site provides a look at Edison and AC power, his engineering choices, and his legacy as a master in product research and development. Find out more.

Access this Web site from http://www.myreportlinks.com

ten years. He made an excellent storage battery that was nearly indestructible. Unfortunately, people did not want to buy electric cars. Carmakers had already made cheap gasoline-powered cars. Their cars were smellier and noisier than Edison's electric car. Edison was truly ahead of his time. This is what he had to say about his battery: "It is of enormous importance because of the shortage of gasoline . . . liquid fuel from the earth is limited in quantity."[9] One hundred years later, these words ring true. Carmakers are just now putting electric cars on the market.

A HERO FOR ALL TIMES

As Edison neared the end of his life, his pace slowed. He was used to working sixteen hours a day. He often said that people did not need so much sleep. Now he began to sleep more. Other people retire in their old age, but not Edison. He always kept busy. He followed the progress of science with great interest. Even during his dying days, he asked questions about work at the laboratory.

CHAPTER

6

➜ CEMENT HOUSES FOR YOU AND ME

Edison sunk many millions of dollars into his iron mine in the 1890s. He had invented an iron ore processor. It was a machine that could remove iron from other crushed rock. The machine used powerful magnets. Mining experts were not impressed. They tried to warn Edison that his idea was not cost-effective. Then a better source of iron was discovered in the Mesabi Range of Minnesota and iron prices fell. The iron ore mine was a failure. Edison lost millions of dollars. He did not take it to heart. He found new uses for the mine's machinery. He started making cement. Yankee Stadium is made from Edison cement.

Thomas Edison's Concrete Houses

AmericanHeritage.com
History's Homepage

Login | Register | Subscribe
Make this your homepage

Home | People | Places | Events | Entertainment | Magazine | Invention & Technology | Travel | Blog | Discussions

Search | Search Our Invention & Technology Article Archives | Invention & Technology ▼ | Search

Most Popular Searches: Thomas Jefferson | September 11 | NASA | Baseball | American Revolution

Invention & Technology Magazine   Winter 1996 Volume 11, Issue 3

Browse Archives

Browse our *Invention & Technology* Magazine issues from 1985 to the present.

Archives >>

Browse by Feature

Forbes Collector
Immigration in America
American Heritage

THOMAS EDISON'S CONCRETE HOUSES

THE WIZARD OF MENLO PARK thought instant homes of concrete poured in molds could clear out America's slums
BY MICHAEL PETERSON

"I AM GOING TO LIVE TO SEE THE DAY WHEN A WORKING MAN'S HOUSE can be built of concrete in a week. ... If I succeed, it will take from the city slums everybody who is worth taking." When Thomas Edison announced in 1906 that he planned to recast the world and mold it according to his own vision, people took him at his word. He was already well on his way to becoming history's most successful and productive visionary, and with the progress that he had recently made in the Portland cement industry, the prospect of concrete houses was not at all extraordinary. The

Swim
at Home
All the Benefits of

Edison had an idea for inexpensive prefabricated cement houses made from molds. Find out more about the inventor's concept when you visit this site.

Access this Web site from http://www.myreportlinks.com

In thinking of new inventions, Edison often thought about how he could help people. Edison did not like city slums because they were dirty and rundown. People lived in bad conditions there. Edison thought affordable houses in the countryside would be better. After all, people who had the money could live outside of the city. They took the daily train into the city for work. What if he could make cheap houses? Poor people could afford to live in the country, too. Edison used his cement to build houses. He built molds for the walls and roofs out of steel. Then he poured cement into the molds. The cement took a few days to dry. When it was dry, the builders removed the molds. All the builders had to do was add windows and doors. The idea never caught on. Why not? People said they did not want houses that all looked the same.[1]

→ A MARTYR TO SCIENCE

In 1895, a scientist from Germany saw something strange. He found a new kind of light ray. When he shone the ray at his hand, he could see his bones through his flesh. William Roentgen had discovered the X-ray. X stood for unknown. He told the world of his discovery. Edison read the news and grew excited. What could X-rays be used for? How could they help people? Soon Edison and his workers

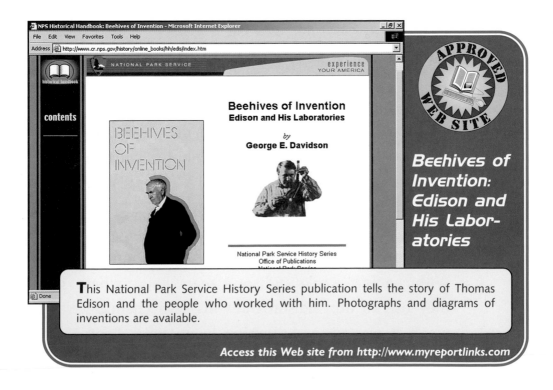

NPS Historical Handbook: Beehives of Invention - Microsoft Internet Explorer

File   Edit   View   Favorites   Tools   Help

Address   http://www.cr.nps.gov/history/online_books/hh/edis/index.htm

NATIONAL PARK SERVICE

experience
YOUR AMERICA

historical handbook

contents

Beehives of Invention
Edison and His Laboratories

by
George E. Davidson

BEEHIVES OF INVENTION

National Park Service History Series
Office of Publications

Done

Beehives of Invention: Edison and His Laboratories

This National Park Service History Series publication tells the story of Thomas Edison and the people who worked with him. Photographs and diagrams of inventions are available.

Access this Web site from http://www.myreportlinks.com

were using X-rays at the West Orange laboratory. They exposed themselves to X-rays over and over again. No one knew how dangerous X-rays could be. One man used X-rays more than the other workers. His name was Clarence Dally. After a time, Dally knew something was wrong. The X-rays had burned him badly and his skin did not heal. He had cancer. It spread throughout his body. Dally died seven years later. Today we know much more about X-rays. Doctors and dentists use them safely. X-rays help them to cure sick and injured people.

A War Hero

A great war broke out in 1914. It would become known as World War I. America did not take sides, not at first. Even so, the war made life hard in America. Edison had a tough time. He could not get the chemicals he needed from Europe. Edison looked for a new supply. No matter whom he spoke with, the answer was the same: the chemicals would not be ready for months. Edison thought long and hard. He hired scientists who worked in three shifts. They worked all day and night. Edison was in charge of the entire operation. He slept on a bench in the laboratory. Within a few weeks, Edison's team knew what they had to do.[2] Edison built his own chemical plant. It was up and running in no time. Soon other people were asking Edison for help. He went

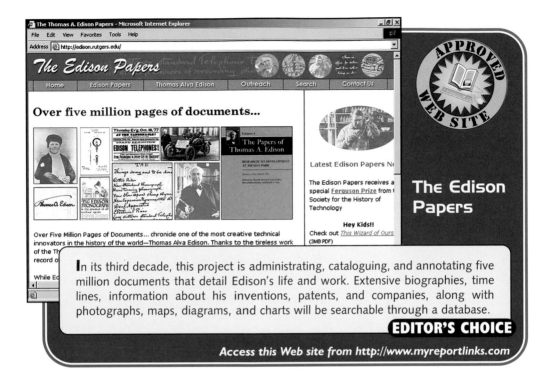

The Edison Papers

The Thomas A. Edison Papers - Microsoft Internet Explorer

File   Edit   View   Favorites   Tools   Help

Address http://edison.rutgers.edu/

The Edison Papers

| Home | Edison Papers | Thomas Alva Edison | Outreach | Search | Contact Us |

Over five million pages of documents...

The Papers of
Thomas A. Edison

RESEARCH TO DEVELOPMENT
AT MENLO PARK

Latest Edison Papers N

The Edison Papers receives a
special **Ferguson Prize** from t
Society for the History of
Technology

Hey Kids!!
Check out *This Wizard of Ours*
(3MB PDF)

Over Five Million Pages of Documents... chronicle one of the most creative technical
innovators in the history of the world—Thomas Alva Edison. Thanks to the tireless work
of the Th
record o

While Ed

In its third decade, this project is administrating, cataloguing, and annotating five
million documents that detail Edison's life and work. Extensive biographies, time
lines, information about his inventions, patents, and companies, along with
photographs, maps, diagrams, and charts will be searchable through a database.

EDITOR'S CHOICE

Access this Web site from http://www.myreportlinks.com

into business making chemicals. He built more
plants in Pennsylvania and Alabama.

The United States Navy now approached Edison
to get his ideas. Edison could do whatever he set
his mind to do. He had proved this time and time
again. America was now at war. This world war was
different from past wars. The weapons were more
complex. Science was changing the way nations
fought wars. Could Edison help them to win? Edison
agreed to try. He felt a duty to help his country. He
would be the president of a new team of scientists
called the U.S. Naval Consulting Board. Edison
went right to work. He found a way to detect enemy

From left to right are Thomas Edison, John Burroughs, and Henry Ford at Edison's winter home in Fort Myers, Florida.

torpedoes, but he soon grew frustrated. No one seemed to be listening to his ideas.[3] Edison was not used to that. At his laboratory he was in control. Now the Navy was in charge. Edison came up with many ideas, but the Navy did not use them. Edison preferred to work on his own.

CAMPING TRIPS OF THE RICH AND FAMOUS

Edison had few close friends because he preferred to keep to himself. In his later years, he struck up a friendship with Henry Ford. Ford made a name for himself when he produced the Model T. The Model T was an early car that did not cost too much. Many Americans bought Model Ts. Edison was wary of Ford at first. After all, they were competitors in the car market. But Ford had a great respect for Edison and viewed him as a role model. When the two men met, Edison saw they had a lot in common. They were both savvy businessmen, and they were both curious about the world around them. Ford asked nearly as many questions as Edison.

Edison talked Ford into going on a camping trip. They spent two weeks touring New England and New York. The famed natural scientist, John Burroughs, also went along. Burroughs was an old man in his eighties. The group toured the countryside by car while a car full of servants and a cook followed behind. The men set up their tents in fields and they cooked over a campfire. Edison insisted that none of the men shave. They were roughing it, after all. There were more camping trips other years. After Burroughs died, Edison invited other famous men along. Harvey Firestone joined the group. Firestone made his fortune by making tires for cars. One year, the president of the United States even joined them. President Warren Harding was a friend of Firestone. What a sight they must have been, all those rich, famous men camping on the side of the road. After a few

Welcome To The Edison & Ford Winter Estates Web Site! - Microsoft Internet Explorer

File   Edit   View   Favorites   Tools   Help

Address http://www.efwefla.org/

Edison & Ford
Winter Estates
Welcome to the Edison & Ford Winter Estates located in sunny Fort Myers, Florida.

"Fools call wise men fools. A wise man never calls any man a fool." - Thomas Edison

APPROVED WEB SITE

Website

Thomas Edison and Henry Ford owned neighboring properties in Florida that acted as their winter residences. When you visit the **Edison and Ford Winter Estates** Web site, you can see pictures of the homes and botanical gardens. Biographies of both men are available, along with some of their most famous quotes.

The Edison Building in Greenfield Village, Dearborn, Michigan. It is part of The Henry Ford museum.

years, they abandoned the camping trips. Word spread from town to town that the group was on its way. People came out to greet them. Cameras flashed. Journalists asked questions for their stories. Edison had enough. He spent his free time in Fort Myers, Florida. He owned a winter house in a secluded spot there.

SEARCH FOR RUBBER

Americans were crazy about automobiles. Factories churned out cars as fast as they could. During and after the war it was hard to get rubber. Car tires were made from rubber that came from the sap of plants. Rubber plants do not grow in the United States because the climate is not right. They grow in the tropics. Most rubber came to America from the jungles of Malaysia, a country in Asia. The British were in control of the rubber from Malaysia. Ford and Firestone wanted a new source of rubber. Could rubber come from another plant? Could rubber be made in the United States? They asked their friend Edison. Plants were not his area of expertise, but Edison loved to solve problems. He set out to learn all he could about plants.

In 1923, he began looking for a new source of rubber. He turned 9 acres (4 hectares) of land near his Florida home into fields. He grew different plants and tried to make rubber from their sap.

One plant, the common weed goldenrod, was promising. Edison grew a very tall strain of goldenrod. However, he did not find a good source before he died. Not long after his death, people found a way to make synthetic rubber. Synthetic rubber is not from plants; it is man-made.

⊜ GOLDEN JUBILEE OF LIGHT

The year was 1929. Fifty years had passed since Edison made his lightbulb. Henry Ford planned a tribute to his friend. He invited Edison and his wife to attend a party. It would be a celebration of Edison and his work. Ford called it the Golden Jubilee of Light. Ford had just opened a new museum of history, now called simply The Henry Ford. He built it near his factory in Dearborn, Michigan. He wanted people to learn about history in a new way. He would show history in action. For one of the exhibits, Ford had rebuilt the Menlo Park laboratory. He paid close attention to detail; he wanted it to look just like the original. He even brought dirt from New Jersey to put outside the door. The museum was the perfect place for the Golden Jubilee.

The night of the party had come. Edison moved slowly as his wife held his arm. Then Edison saw his old laboratory from so many years ago. He sat down in a chair, lost in his thoughts. There were tears in his eyes. "There is only one thing," he told Ford. "The floor was never this clean."[4] Then Edison made a lightbulb, just as he had fifty years earlier. A few of his friends and workers from the old days were there to help. People at home listened on their radios. President Herbert Hoover was there to watch. Then came a grand banquet. For a minute, Edison said he would not go in. He was too tired and it had been an emotional night. He sat and took a rest. In the end, he took his place of honor at the head table. There were many important people there who wanted to praise Edison. They gave speech after speech, but Edison could not hear them.[5] He was too hard of hearing. He stood and read a speech. When he was done, he collapsed in his chair. He had passed out. When he came to, he asked to go home. The evening with all its glory was over.

A Fitting Tribute

On October 18, 1931, Edison died peacefully. His health had been poor for the past few years. He had diabetes. Edison tried to heal himself by going on a milk diet. For years he ate no food, but drank a glass of milk every few hours. Milk could not give his body enough nutrition, and he lost weight and grew weak. On October 14, 1931, he slipped into a coma. The world was sorry to lose a great hero. Americans wanted to

Always a tireless worker, Edison punches the clock on his seventy-fourth birthday.

©T.A.E.
2-11-21

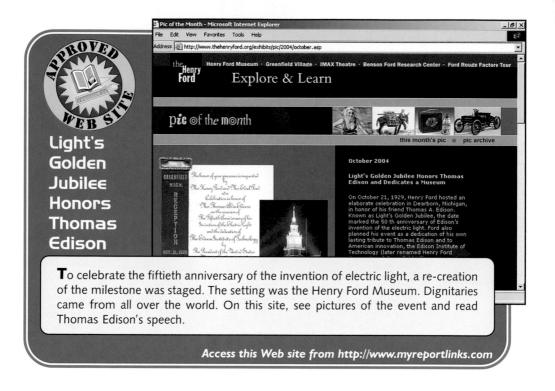

Light's Golden Jubilee Honors Thomas Edison

Pic of the Month - Microsoft Internet Explorer

File   Edit   View   Favorites   Tools   Help

Address http://www.thehenryford.org/exhibits/pic/2004/october.asp

the Henry Ford

Henry Ford Museum · Greenfield Village · IMAX Theatre · Benson Ford Research Center · Ford Rouge Factory Tour

Explore & Learn

pic of the month

this month's pic ◉ pic archive

October 2004

Light's Golden Jubilee Honors Thomas Edison and Dedicates a Museum

On October 21, 1929, Henry Ford hosted an elaborate celebration in Dearborn, Michigan, in honor of his friend Thomas A. Edison. Known as Light's Golden Jubilee, the date marked the 50 th anniversary of Edison's invention of the electric light. Ford also planned his event as a dedication of his own lasting tribute to Thomas Edison and to American innovation, the Edison Institute of Technology (later renamed Henry Ford

To celebrate the fiftieth anniversary of the invention of electric light, a re-creation of the milestone was staged. The setting was the Henry Ford Museum. Dignitaries came from all over the world. On this site, see pictures of the event and read Thomas Edison's speech.

Access this Web site from http://www.myreportlinks.com

mark the passing of the famous inventor from this world. All over America, people turned off their lights. For one minute the nation was dark. Then the lights came back on. The world was a brighter place, thanks to that hard working man, Thomas Alva Edison.

ACTIVITIES TO TRY YOURSELF

Have you ever dreamed of becoming an inventor? Edison often said it was not his genius that made him a great inventor but his dedication and hard work. If Edison was right, then anyone who is willing to work hard can be a successful inventor. It is never too early to start thinking like an inventor. Inventors ask lots of questions. They like to know why things happen.

People like to tell a story about Edison when he was six years old. Young Al wondered why a mother goose sat on her eggs. He was told she was keeping them warm so they could hatch. Al decided to try an experiment. His family later found him in a pile of straw in the barn. He was sitting on some eggs. He wanted to see if he could hatch goslings, too.[1] The point of the story is Edison was always curious. He wanted to figure things out for himself, and he was not afraid of looking foolish.

● ●

⊜ PERFORMING YOUR OWN EXPERIMENTS

Edison made his first laboratory in his bedroom. His mother was not thrilled. The chemicals were messy. His parents made him move his laboratory into the basement. He tried experiments he read in a school textbook. Not all of Edison's early

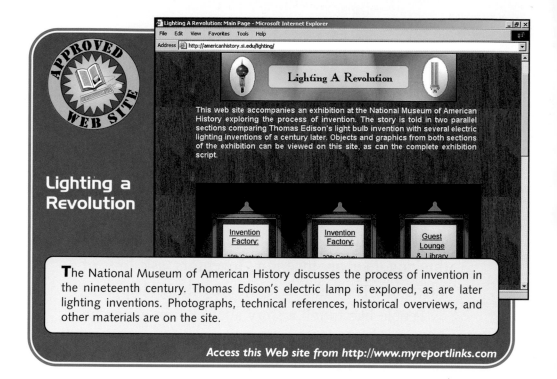

Lighting a Revolution

Lighting A Revolution: Main Page - Microsoft Internet Explorer

File   Edit   View   Favorites   Tools   Help

Address http://americanhistory.si.edu/lighting/

Lighting A Revolution

This web site accompanies an exhibition at the National Museum of American History exploring the process of invention. The story is told in two parallel sections comparing Thomas Edison's light bulb invention with several electric lighting inventions of a century later. Objects and graphics from both sections of the exhibition can be viewed on this site, as can the complete exhibition script.

Invention Factory: | Invention Factory: | Guest Lounge & Library

The National Museum of American History discusses the process of invention in the nineteenth century. Thomas Edison's electric lamp is explored, as are later lighting inventions. Photographs, technical references, historical overviews, and other materials are on the site.

Access this Web site from http://www.myreportlinks.com

experiments were good ones. Once he started a fire in his father's barn. He said he had wanted to see what would happen. What happened? The barn burned down. Young Al's father was very angry.[2] There is a lesson to be learned there. If your experiment could be dangerous, check with your parents. Ask for permission and help.

Edison was always writing and sketching. He filled thirty-five hundred notebooks with his ideas. If you stacked up all of Edison's papers, the stack would be taller than the Empire State Building.[3] Every time he performed an experiment, he took detailed notes. His notes helped him keep track of what he learned. He could also use them as a record of when he had an idea. In his field of work, Edison needed to be able to prove when he had an idea. Ideas were his bread and butter. His notebooks helped him protect his ideas from theft. Before you begin the experiments in this chapter, find a notebook. Keep track of what you do. Write down what you use, and what you think might happen. After you do your experiment, jot down the results. What would you do differently next time? Did it raise other questions for you to explore?

MAGNETISM AND ELECTRICITY

We use electricity every day. It makes machines work. But what exactly is electricity? Electricity is a force. It is found in nature. You can make electricity. Have you ever scuffed your feet on a carpet? When you touched something, you felt a zap. That zap was a form of electricity. It is called static electricity. Static means "stationary," or not moving.

Activity #1

Static Electricity

You will need a sweater, a balloon, and some tiny scraps of paper. Blow up the balloon and rub it on your sweater. This will give your balloon an electric charge. Now hold the balloon near the tiny scraps of paper. Slowly move the balloon back and forth. What happens to the paper pieces? The balloon acts as a weak magnet. Experiment to see what else the balloon can pick up. What happens if you put the

▲ Edison mixes a concoction in his lab.

balloon near your hair? What happens when you place the balloon on the wall? Does it stay in place or does it fall to the ground? Set the balloon aside for ten minutes. Does the balloon still hold its electric charge? Is it still charged after half an hour?

Why does the balloon act like that? To find the answer, we need to think about the balloon on a microscopic level. The balloon is matter. The pieces of paper are also matter. Everything you can see around you is matter. Even you are matter. What is matter? Matter is made up of atoms. Atoms are tiny—our eyes cannot see them without a powerful microscope. They may be invisible, but they are very real. Electrons, neutrons, and protons are parts of an atom. Neutrons and protons move in the center of each atom. Electrons are negatively charged and move around the outside of an atom. Protons have a positive charge. Neutrons do not have a charge. When you rubbed the balloon on your sweater, the balloon picked up electrons. The balloon then had extra electrons. Matter with extra electrons "carries a charge." The charged balloon needed more protons to get rid of its charge. When you held the charged balloon near the paper, it attracted the positive protons in the pieces of paper. A balloon cannot hold a charge for long.

🧪 MAKING A MAGNET

You will need a magnet, a sewing needle, and some metal paper clips. First of all, use the magnet to pick up the paper clips. Your magnet needs to be strong enough to pick them up easily. Now place the needle near the paper clips. Does anything happen? Can you pick up a paper clip with the needle? Now stroke the needle along the magnet. Always move it in the same direction; do not move it back and forth. Do this fifteen to twenty times. Try again to pick up the paper clips with the needle.

By moving the needle along the magnet, you gave the needle an electric charge. Like the charged balloon in the last experiment, the needle will not hold the charge for long. The charge is temporary. An electric generator works in a similar way. There is a powerful magnet inside the generator. When the generator is turned on, wires move rapidly through along the magnet's field. The wires pick up electrons. They become charged. This charge is what we call electricity.

ACTIVITY #3

🧪 MAKING A SIMPLE COMPASS

You will need a bowl of water, a rectangle of sturdy paper small enough to float on the water in the bowl, and the needle from the last experiment. Float the paper on the surface of the water. Carefully lay the *charged* needle on the surface of the paper. If your needle holds a charge, it will begin to spin. If it is not spinning, you may want to test the needle. Does it still hold a charge? Will it pick up a paper clip? You can always recharge it. Stroke it along the magnet again. What makes the paper spin? The needle is looking for the earth's North Pole. A free-moving needle with a magnetic charge will always point north. Our planet is a huge magnet. Like all magnets, Earth has a north and a south pole. Your magnet is aligning itself to the earth's powerful magnetic field.

• •

⊖ CHEMISTRY

Edison made his mark on the world with his advances in electricity. His true love, however, was chemistry. "Grand science, chemistry. I like it best of all the sciences," Edison admitted.[4] Chemistry is an essential science. Chemists are the scientists who study this field of science. Chemists learn what makes up substances and investigate what happens when a substance is mixed with another substance. Chemistry is the study of atoms and how atoms bond to form different molecules.

▲ *A photograph of Edison in his laboratory that was taken around 1911.*

Activity #4

🧪 KITCHEN CHEMISTRY

You will need an onion, a plastic knife, and a cutting board. Begin by peeling the onion. Now chop it into fine pieces. Molecules from the onion are now floating in the air. Are your eyes smarting? You may even be crying. Why? When the onion molecules reach your eyes, there is a chemical reaction. The onion's molecules and the salty water on the surface of your eyes are reacting. Together they form sulfuric acid. This acid irritates your eyes. Your eyes form tears. The tears will wash away the acid.

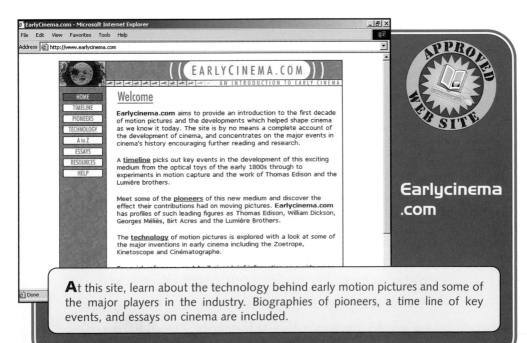

At this site, learn about the technology behind early motion pictures and some of the major players in the industry. Biographies of pioneers, a time line of key events, and essays on cinema are included.

Access this Web site from http://www.myreportlinks.com

Activity #5

PLAYING A TRICK ON YOUR EYES

You will need a 2-inch (5 centimeter) round disk of cardboard, a one-foot (.3 meter) length of string, a marker, and some glue. On the left-hand side of the cardboard disk, write the letters "EDI." Now flip the disk over. On the right-hand side of the cardboard disk, write the letters "SON." Now glue the string horizontally across the disk. It should lie along the middle of one side of the disk. Wait for the glue to dry. Hold onto the ends of the string. Twirl the string rapidly. The disk will flip from side to side. Do you see the full word "Edison"? That is because each image remains in your brain for about $1/16$ of a second. When you flip the disk from side to side, your brain cannot tell the difference between the two separate images

• •

⮕ EXPERIMENT WITH WHAT YOU KNOW

When Edison was young, he learned all he could about the telegraph. He was curious: How did it work? Once he understood how it worked, he wondered how it could work better. He just knew he could improve the telegraph. He did, too. You can follow Edison's example. If you think of a better way to do something, act on it. As Edison would say, invention is one percent inspiration and ninety-nine percent perspiration. The work to make your idea happen is the hard part. The rewards are great. Good inventions can change the future.

Report Links

The Internet sites described below can be accessed at
http://www.myreportlinks.com

▶**Edison National Historic Site**
Editor's Choice This National Park Service Web site commemorates Thomas Edison.

▶**Edison Invents!**
Editor's Choice Learn more about the creative genius of Edison on this site.

▶**The Edison Papers**
Editor's Choice Rutgers University has cataloged the papers of Thomas Edison at this site.

▶**Thomas Edison and the Menlo Park Laboratory**
Editor's Choice The Henry Ford museum offers an exhibit on Thomas Edison and his lab.

▶**Inventing Entertainment**
Editor's Choice This collection focuses on Edison's contributions to motion pictures.

▶*Edison's Miracle of Light*
Editor's Choice This PBS site commemorates the man who helped to harness electricity.

▶**Alexander Graham Bell National Historic Site of Canada**
Read about Bell's history and review a chronology of his life on this site.

▶*Beehives of Invention: Edison and His Laboratories*
Full-length version of e-book on Edison.

▶**The Charles Edison Fund**
This site is dedicated to the genius of Thomas Edison.

▶**Earlycinema.com**
This Web site offers an introduction to early cinema.

▶**Edison After Forty**
Take an online pictorial tour of Edison's professional and family life.

▶**Edison and Ford Winter Estates**
Take a tour and learn more about two of America's greatest business tycoons.

▶**The Edison Birthplace Museum**
Take an online tour of Edison's first home.

▶*Edison, His Life and Inventions*
This site offers a full-text electronic book about Edison that was written in 1910.

▶**Electrification**
This is a history of electricity.

Report Links

The Internet sites described below can be accessed at
http://www.myreportlinks.com

▶**Frank L. Pope**
A biography of the nineteenth century telegrapher and electrical engineer.

▶**A History of Electric Lighting in the Home**
This Institution of Engineering and Technology Web site explores electric lighting.

▶**History of the Electric Power Industry**
This Edison Electric Institute site tracts the evolution of electricity.

▶**History of the Stock Ticker**
This is an interesting and in-depth look at the invention of the stock ticker.

▶**History of Wire and Broadcast Communication**
This FCC history of telecommunications covers a period of 150 years.

▶**The Invention Factory: Thomas Edison's Laboratories**
Students will be challenged when they visit this National Park Service Cultural Resource site.

▶**Lighting a Revolution**
This online exhibition reviews the process of inventing.

▶**Light's Golden Jubilee Honors Thomas Edison**
Henry Ford's tribute to Thomas Edison.

▶**Michael Faraday**
This is a biography of Michael Faraday, the British scientist.

▶**Mina Miller Edison Collection**
The Chautauqua Institution presents this Edison archival collection.

▶*A School Compendium of Natural and Experimental Philosophy*
Read the book that changed the course of Edison's life.

▶**Teaching With Documents**
Learn about the inventions of Thomas Edison and Alexander Graham Bell.

▶**Thomas Alva Edison**
Mississippi State University offers this site on Edison's contributions to electrical engineering.

▶**Thomas Edison's Concrete Houses**
American Heritage magazine has an article on Edison's vision for the future of homes.

▶**United States Patent and Trademark Office**
This government Web site offers step-by-step instructions on how to register a patent.

arc lamp—An early electric light that could only be used outdoors.

atom—A tiny piece of matter too little to see with the bare eye.

burner—The part of a lightbulb that glows.

carbon—A chemical element found in coal and charcoal.

chemistry—A field of science that studies what matter is and how it reacts.

compass—A tool with a magnetic needle that points north.

current—The flow of electricity.

duplex—An improved telegraph that sent two messages at a time.

electron—A part of an atom that has a negative electric charge.

friction—The force made when two things rub together.

generator—A machine that makes electricity.

incandesce—To heat something until it glows.

invent—To make something no one has ever made before.

kinetoscope—An early kind of movie camera.

legislator—A person who makes laws; a member of the legislature.

magnet—A metal or ore that attracts iron and steel.

matter—Everything that takes up space.

Morse code—The dots and dashes that stand for letters in a telegraph message.

oxygen—A gas found in earth's air.

patent—A legal document that states an inventor owns the rights to an invention.

phonograph—The first machine to record a sound and play it back.

platinum—A valuable silver metal that does not melt easily.

pole—Either end of a magnet where the pull is the strongest.

proton—A part of an atom that has a positive electric charge.

quadruplex—An improved telegraph that could send four messages at once.

roll call—When someone shouts out each of the names of a group of people.

rubber—An elastic-like substance made from the sap of plants.

static electricity—An electric charge made by friction.

stock ticker—A machine that gets updates about the changing price of gold.

telegraph—A way of sending messages over a wire.

vacuum—A space that is empty of all matter.

X-ray—A powerful beam of light that can go through skin.

Chapter 1. The Wizard of Menlo Park

1. Jill Jonnes, *Empires of Light* (New York: Random House, 2003), p. 66.

2. Wyn Wachhorst, *Thomas Alva Edison: An American Myth* (Cambridge, Mass.: MIT Press, 1981), pp. 23–26.

3. Neil Baldwin, *Edison: Inventing the Century* (New York: Hyperion, 1995), p. 84.

4. Ronald W. Clark, *Edison: The Man Who Made the Future* (New York: G.P. Putnam's Sons, 1977), p. 214.

Chapter 2. "What Seems Impossible Today May Not Be Tomorrow"

1. Neil Baldwin, *Edison: Inventing the Century* (New York: Hyperion, 1995), pp. 4–5.

2. Paul Israel, *Edison: A Life of Invention* (New York: John Wiley & Sons, Inc., 1998), p. 15.

3. Thomas Alva Edison, as quoted in Ronald W. Clark, *Edison: The Man Who Made the Future* (New York: G.P. Putnam's Sons, 1977), p. 9.

4. Thomas Alva Edison, as quoted in Israel, pp. 14–15.

5. Thomas Alva Edison, as quoted in Clark, p. 12.

6. Thomas Alva Edison, as quoted in Theresa M. Collins and Lisa Gitelman, eds., *Thomas Edison and Modern America: A Brief History with Documents* (New York: Palgrave, 2002), p. 42.

7. Ibid. p. 40.

Chapter 3. "I Am Going to Hustle . . ."

1. Thomas Alva Edison, as quoted in Theresa

M. Collins and Lisa Gitelman, eds., *Thomas Edison and Modern America: A Brief History with Documents* (New York: Palgrave, 2002), pp. 45–46.

2. Francis Arthur Jones, *Thomas Alva Edison* (New York: Thomas Y. Crowell & Co., 1924), p. 64.

3. Robert A. Conot, *A Streak of Luck: The Life and Legend of Thomas Alva Edison* (New York: Seaview Books, 1979), pp. 31–32.

4. Thomas Alva Edison, as quoted in Collins and Gitelman, eds., pp. 55–56.

5. Ronald W. Clark, *Edison: The Man Who Made the Future* (New York: G.P. Putnam's Sons, 1977), p. 28.

6. Conot, pp. 47–48.

7. Neil Baldwin, *Edison: Inventing the Century* (New York: Hyperion, 1995), p. 134.

8. Clark, pp. 67–68.

9. Paul Israel, *Edison: A Life of Invention* (New York: John Wiley & Sons, Inc., 1998), p. 192.

Chapter 4. "Invention is One Percent Inspiration and 99% Perspiration."

1. Thomas A. Edison, "Edison's Newest Marvel," *New York Sun,* September 16, 1878 as quoted in Theresa M. Collins and Lisa Gitelman, eds., *Thomas Edison and Modern America: A Brief History with Documents* (New York: Palgrave, 2002), p. 84.

2. Ronald W. Clark, *Edison: The Man Who Made the Future* (New York: G.P. Putnam's Sons, 1977), p. 90.

3. Robert A. Conot, *A Streak of Luck: The Life and Legend of Thomas Alva Edison* (New York: Seaview Books, 1979), pp. 133–134.

4. Byron M. Vanderbilt, *Thomas Edison, Chemist* (Washington, D.C.: American Chemical Society, 1971), p. 43.

5. Ira Flatow, *They All Laughed . . .* (New York: HarperCollins, 1992), p. 17.

6. Wyn Wachhorst, *Thomas Alva Edison: An American Myth* (Cambridge, Mass.: MIT Press, 1981), pp. 42–43.

7. Edward H. Johnson, "Edison Electric Light Stock Considered as a Speculative Holding for the Ensuing Quarter," *Draft Report for Investors,* September 1881, as quoted in Collins and Gitelman, eds., p. 118.

8. Richard Moran, *Executioner's Current: Thomas Edison, George Westinghouse, and the Invention of the Electric Chair* (New York: Alfred A. Knopf, 2002), p. 43.

9. George E. Davidson, *Beehives of Invention: Edison and his Laboratories* (Washington, D.C.: National Park Service, 1973), p. 34.

Chapter 5. Inventing Things That Would Sell

1. Ronald W. Clark, *Edison: The Man Who Made the Future* (New York: G.P. Putnam's Sons, 1977), p. 57.

2. Neil Baldwin, *Edison: Inventing the Century* (New York: Hyperion, 1995), p. 73.

3. Paul Israel, *Edison: A Life of Invention* (New York: John Wiley & Sons, Inc., 1998), p. 144.

4. Thomas Edison, as quoted in Robert Conot, *A Streak of Luck: the Life and Legend of Thomas Alva Edison* (New York: Seaview Books, 1979), p. 323.

5. George E. Davidson, *Beehives of Invention: Edison and his Laboratories* (Washington, D.C.: National Park Service, 1973), p. 52.

6. Ira Flatow, *They All Laughed . . .* (New York: HarperCollins, 1992), p. 37.

7. Thomas A. Edison, as quoted in Collins and Gitelman, eds., *Thomas Edison and Modern America: A Brief History with Documents* (New York: Palgrave, 2002), p. 143.

8. Richard Moran, *Executioner's Current: Thomas Edison, George Westinghouse, and the Invention of the Electric Chair* (New York: Alfred A. Knopf, 2002), pp. 57–58, 101–102.

9. Francis Arthur Jones, *Thomas Alva Edison* (New York: Thomas Y. Crowell & Co., 1924), p. 260.

Chapter 6. A Hero for All Times

1. Grand Rapids Evening Press, "Edison's Poured Cement Houses Here," *Grand Rapids Evening Press,* July 9, 1909 as quoted in Theresa M. Collins and Lisa Gitelman, eds., *Thomas Edison and Modern America* (New York: Palgrave, 2002), p. 159.

2. Ronald W. Clark, *Edison: The Man Who Made the Future* (New York: G.P. Putnam's Sons, 1977), pp. 217–218.

3. Robert A. Conot, *A Streak of Luck: The Life and Legend of Thomas Alva Edison* (New York: Seaview Books, 1979), pp. 417–418.

4. Clark, p. 240.

5. Wyn Wachhorst, *Thomas Alva Edison: An American Myth* (Cambridge, Mass.: MIT Press, 1981), p. 168.

Activities to Try Yourself

1. Francis Arthur Jones, *Thomas Alva Edison* (New York: Thomas Y. Crowell & Co., 1924), p. 10.

2. Robert A. Conot, *A Streak of Luck: The Life and Legend of Thomas Alva Edison* (New York: Seaview Books, 1979), p. 5.

3. Editors of the Thomas A. Edison Papers, "This Wizard of Ours," *Rutgers Science,* n.d., <http://edison.rutgers.edu/thiswizard.pdf> (March 4, 2006).

4. James G. Cook and the Thomas Alva Edison Foundation, *The Thomas Edison Book of Easy and Incredible Experiments* (New York: John Wiley & Sons, 1988), p. 59.

Adair, Gene. *Thomas Alva Edison: Inventing the Electric Age*. New York: Oxford University Press, 1996.

Bender, Lionel. *Eyewitness: Invention*. New York: DK Publishing, 2000.

Cramer, Carol, ed. *Thomas Edison*. San Diego, Calif.: Greenwood Press, 2001.

Good, Keith. *Zap It! Exciting Electricity Activities*. Minneapolis: Lerner Publications, 1999.

Hopping, Lorraine Egan. I*nventors and Inventions*. New York: Scholastic, 1999.

Macaulay, David. *The New Way Things Work*. Boston: Houghton Mifflin, 1998.

Sproule, Anna. *Thomas A. Edison: the World's Greatest Inventor*. Woodbridge, Conn.: Blackbirch Press, 2000.

Tagliaferro, Linda. *Thomas Edison: Inventor of the Age of Electricity*. Minneapolis: Lerner Publications, 2003.

Wallace, Joseph. *The Light Bulb*. New York: Atheneum Books for Young Readers, 1999.

Wulffson, Don L. *The Kid Who Invented the Trampoline: More Surprising Stories about Inventions*. New York: Dutton Books, 2001.